I0188393

OOPS!

The Art of Learning from Mistakes and Adventures

Kent Sterling

A Kent Sterling Publication

Terre Haute, IN

Oops! © 2019 Kent Sterling
Hard cover EAN-ISBN-13: 978-1-7342074-0-8
Paperback EAN-ISBN-13: 978-1-7342074-1-5
E -book EAN-ISBN-13: 978-1-7342074-2-2

All rights reserved under International and Pan-American Copyright Conventions

No part of this book may be reproduced, stored in a database or other retrieval system, or transmitted in any form, by any means, including mechanical, photocopy, recording or otherwise, without the prior written permission of the publisher.

Cover design by Phil Velikan
Cover art ©devlyanthi79/shutterstock

Packaged by Wish Publishing

Printed in the United States of America
10 9 8 7 6 5 4 3 2 1

This book is dedicated to my mom, dad, sister, wife, son, extended family and friends who have continued to love, like or tolerate me as a flawed human being despite being incapable of learning in a conventional way. Thanks to readers who look past their doubts that any one person could be this relentless in his willingness to err. Each chapter describes an event exactly as it exists in my memory. None are embellished, as they are odd, foolish, funny or horrifying enough as they happened. If you can learn from my screw-ups and not repeat them, all the work in writing this book is worth it.

OOPS!

The Art of Learning from Mistakes and Adventures

Table of Contents

Foreword..9

Using the N-Word for the Only Time.............................13

What do You Study When You Already Know the Answers?............17

Hey, Where's My Present?...22

Fight! Fight! Fight!..26

Candy, Baseball Cards, Dancing and Lessons at White's..............31

Four Fearless Months Bring Out My Best........................36

Can't Hit the Curve..41

Hey Now, You're an All-Star, Get Your Game On, GO PLAY!............46

Chemistry Class for Idiots — Or One Idiot........................51

So You Want to be a Rock 'n' Roll Star.............................58

Painting Providence...65

Turning the Tables on Dad...72

Losing the Roommate Lottery......................................78

Attention Kmart Shoppers!...86

Take the Long Way Home...92

Midnight Mass with the Sterling Family.........................97

Dropping an F-bomb on Eighth Graders........................102

Killing Time at Indiana University................................109

Leaving Harrisburg 117

Welcome to the World — Your Father is a Shoplifter.....................125

Give Us 22 Minutes, We'll Move WMAQ...................................132

Welcome to Second City..137

Welcome to Cafe Dah-mer-ico, May I Take Your Order?.................145

Striking Out with the Family...150

Hoosier Homecoming...156

Pontificating from the Cheap Seats to Get the Colts 165

Desperate and Dateless...169

Making Youth Baseball Fun Again...176

Don't Mess with Riptides..183

Never Bring a Quick Wit to a Gun Fight...................................187

Innocent Hijinx Gone Awry..192

Flowers for MyStar — Or Pranks Burn Bridges...........................199

Dream Comes True by Firing a Great Guy...............................204

Finally my Turn — Fired from Emmis.....................................211

Driving Mr. Boyle...217

Meet Me in St. Louis...225

An Event So Special, It's a Mistake to Write About It....................232

Epilogue..238

Acknowledgements..240

Foreword

I've always given myself a wide berth to make mistakes and learn from them. That's the fun of life, right? No idea where our societal aversion to screwing up came from, but it defies logic. If we prize opportunities to gain knowledge and wisdom — and smart people always say that mistakes are the best teachers — it would seem we should be sprinting toward them rather than hiding from them.

Some high school students I met at a wedding reception a few years ago asked me for life advice. I was totally unprepared for the question, but decided to open my mouth to see what might come out. "Correctable mistakes are fine," I said. "Opiates and pregnancy change lives forever." Neat, tidy, and extemporaneous, that was pretty damn good advice.

I've made mistakes — a lot of them. Having stayed away from heroin and coke, as well as unplanned pregnancy, I've been able to embrace the notion that what doesn't kill us makes us stronger.

This book is a little bit like the scene in the Albert Brooks film, *Defending Your Life*, where a series of idiotic misadventures from Brooks' character's life are shown. In the film it is explained that we are judged for our fears, not missteps. That movie speaks to me. If I screw up and no one is hurt in the process, that's a win. I get to learn a valuable lesson without cost. If that mistake provides an entertaining or uncomfortable memory others find amusing, that's the stuff I can share in a conversation or a book. And this is that book.

Each chapter is a recollection of an episode in my life recalled as they exist in my memory. They are faithful to my memory, and my memory is pretty solid. I'm not some Marilu Henner type who can recall everything from every single day of my life, but what I do remember I can see as though it happened yesterday.

As you read, you might think, "Nobody could be this stupid." I can assure you, I can be — and have been. These aren't all glorious moments, and some were less than pleasant to re-live as I wrote.

At the end of every chapter I've tried to include the lessons those mistakes have provided. The mistakes are funny, sad, or both. And hopefully the lessons are as helpful to you as they have been to me.

I am 57 years old, which means to men and women in their 20s I am irrelevant and incapable of taking meaningful risks that could bring great glory or outrageous shame. My goal is to prove them wrong. Each day brings many opportunities to make an error of commission. I have only just begun to screw up!

Just so you know I'm not writing this book as an exercise to kill time while clicking off the days as a guest of one of America's finer penal institutions, let me tell you a bit about my life other than the errors chronicled here:

My wife is a patient and caring woman with more love in her heart than anyone I've ever met. She is a superb human being who has embraced the ride with me for 32 years of marriage. There have been countless times I have recovered from momentary self-doubt by remembering that Julie must have seen something good. Why argue with her? This book only exists because of her encouragement.

My son Ryan is 31 years old. He's an attorney and former college basketball player who understands how to grind. He has never given Julie and me a reason to question his intellect, moral compass, zest for life, or courage in the face of a tremendous challenge. I tell people that my primary contribution to Ryan's development has been to not screw him up. Many think that's false modesty. Nope. I stand by it. Fundamentally, he is the same person as when he was two.

My parents have always been solid role models, which admittedly raises the question of how I could have been surrounded by so many good people and yet botched things up on so many occasions?

Mom was married at 19, had me at 20, and grew up without a father present in her life. She foundered a bit, and then righted herself to become a beacon of hope for many hundreds of people battling addiction. The adversity Mom has successfully addressed through the past 38 years is her story to tell — not mine. Other than this mention, which is only for context and to voice my sense of pride in her evolution, it will not be discussed. Because she overcame that adversity, she has been able to shepherd those in her care to accept that same challenge.

Dad, the youngest of five children, grew up without a father, but grew into a mature adult. He died in 2002 at the age of 73 having never betrayed a loyalty. Loud, judgmental, and hilarious, Dad was a person people enjoyed being around even if they disliked him. He and his entire family were staunch republicans, while my Mom's family were all Irish-Catholic democrats. My lack of fear in offending others was likely born at holiday dinners where the two families collided.

Idle time in my family was spent preparing to win political arguments, despite the reality that no one actually wins those things. It's ironic that my chosen career began at radio stations where the same arguments happened on — air. The bickering between host, guests, and callers was all too familiar. It might also be why I migrated to sports talk, where debates over quarterbacks, shooting guards, and third basemen are a little more frivolous and fun.

I have worked in talk radio management and as a radio host for the past 30 years. The great thing about talk radio is that every day is different, and the chance for a different challenge exists on a minute by minute basis.

I like a challenge, and I love learning through trial and error (a fact about to become quite clear). If it's difficult, I give it a shot — especially at those things where perfection is impossible. Golf, improvisational comedy, hosting a radio show, marriage, writing, and fatherhood — that's a pretty good start to a list of things I have spent an inordinate amount of time doing and thinking about.

As a final word, I hope these mistakes — foolish (all) and earnest (most) — serve as an example you choose to emulate rather than avoid. Mistakes are good. Embrace them. Share them. Learn and laugh because of them. They should never be a source of shame or regret.

Measuring yourself by your successes is the work of an egomaniac. Take pride in errors of commission. People enjoy someone who reflects with self-deprecation. Self-mockery is charming. Keep your trophies in a closet, but wear your well-intentioned screw-ups like medals!

Using the N-Word for the Only Time

The N-word is a repulsive representation of hatred, bigotry, and stupidity, and I can't remember hearing it until I rode the school bus home for lunch while in the first grade.

My parents were not racists for widely divergent reasons. My mom is inclusive, almost to a fault. She judges everyone through a uniquely positive prism. Dad was different — he always said, "There are so many good reasons to dislike people, I never found race necessary as a tool of judgment." He always said it as though it was a joke, but I always thought he meant it because he lived it.

The school I attended in first grade had no cafeteria, so a school bus would take us to school in the morning, home for lunch, back to school 45 minutes later, and finally home again when the school day ended at 3:15 p.m. One day early in the school year while on the bus ride home for lunch, some fifth graders began to chant, "Tommy is a (N-word)! Tommy is a (N-word)!" [We used the actual word, but I still cannot bring myself to write it here despite it being appropriate to do so.] I joined in without any notion what that word meant. It was a chant, and chanting was fun.

After the third chant, the bus stopped suddenly, and the driver, Reggie, snapped his head around. He pointed at me and two of the fifth graders, "Get off this bus, and you are not allowed to ride on it again!" he shouted. I had no idea what happened — maybe he thought we shouldn't be yelling at Tommy. Eric, John, and I got off the bus and walked the rest of the way home. None of us said a word.

When I got home, I told Mom I was sick and would not be able to go back to school. Mom took my temperature, which was normal despite my best efforts to psychically cause myself to contract an immediate fever. It was obvious to Mom something had gone horribly wrong, and that my illness was fear-based rather than bacterial. I balked at coming clean for a few minutes because I was unsure what I had done or how terrible it was. Finally, I recounted the odd scene in the bus. Mom explained, "Reggie is a black man and that word is used to insult black people. It's a word that is meant to make them feel like they aren't human beings. It's rude and hurtful to use that word."

She went on to explain that Reggie had no clue I didn't know what it meant, and that if I told Reggie I would never use the word again — ever — he would probably allow me to ride again.

So I waited for the bus, and when he opened the door, I told him my mom told me what the word means and that I would never use it again. Reggie waved me onto the bus, and my mom smiled as I took my seat. I didn't use that word again, on the bus or off. And I still haven't.

The funny thing about growing up in an entirely white town like Lake Bluff, Illinois, is that it never occurred to me that racism even existed. My entire awareness of blacks was limited to Chicago athletes like Ernie Banks, Billy Williams, Gale Sayers, and Bob Love, and an elderly man named Alfonse who bagged groceries at Janowitz.

Alfonse was the coolest. He always spoke to me as we waited for our turn at the cashier. He would ask me the same question every week. "Are you going to the Monday night meeting at the First National Bank of Lake Forest?" I would plead with Dad to go to the bank meeting that week. I was convinced this financial conclave would be a life-changing event. I fantasized about these bank meetings as a 17-year-old imagines his first trip to a strip club. Dad would look at me like I was insane, say no, and I would tell Alfonse that we might be able to go next week. This went on until Janowitz closed and was replaced by a Jewel store, and I stopped seeing Alfonse. Never once did we go to the bank for the meeting. I'm not sure Alfonse went to the bank meetings either, but I was always convinced it would have been incredible.

As Mom explained how hurtful it was for people to hear that word, I thought about how it would hurt Alfonse's feelings if I said it to him.

Whether I'm writing, talking, or helping others communicate by writing or talking, it's important to realize that there are two participants in any communication — the deliverer and the recipient. Choosing words that convey the intended meaning is a lot easier said than done.

Who knew that the lesson that would stick in a profound way for me as a first grader wouldn't come from a teacher in a classroom, but from a bus driver who got tired of hearing kids chant what I think is the ugliest word in our language. Learning the lesson that words need to be chosen with care was a gift for me from Reggie the bus driver.

I haven't always been perfect in choosing words, but I've always tried to say what I wanted people to hear so my thought would be clear. Words have the power to make people think, laugh, believe, and empower. They can hurt, anger, and challenge too. Great writers and speakers can capture wondrous and tragic moments in ways that remain etched in our minds forever. That's the greatest challenge in traditional and social media. Using the right words in the right way allows a reader or listener to feel exactly what the writer or speaker feels.

Learning the importance and power of words through being tossed off a school bus during a time of political and racial strife was painful in the moment, but one of the most important lessons of my life.

The right words at the right moment can change minds, and if enough minds are changed, the world changes.

Lessons learned:

1. Words define us.

2. Just because people are chanting something doesn't mean you should.

3. A sincere apology accompanied by a promise of better behavior is difficult to refuse.

4. When people hear something other than what you say, at least part of the blame is yours.

What do You Study When You Already Know the Answers?

"Mrs. Georgevich, why can't I finish writing my sentences as quickly as David Jamieson?" I asked my fourth grade teacher.

Mrs. Georgevich answered in a steely Tommy Lee Jones in *The Fugitive* staccato, "Because – *you...don't...concentrate!*"

She was right, I didn't concentrate. I didn't have to concentrate. I was also told by almost every elementary teacher who had the misfortunate to draw me as a student that I lacked self-control. That was not true. I had excellent self-control. It was the teachers who had little control — over me. My lack of obedience was a conscious choice.

I cannot remember a time when I couldn't read. Mom tells a story about a drive north of Chicago on the Edens Expressway when I was 18 months old. The way she tells it, I asked my parents if we were going to Old Orchard, and then if we were going to Lake Avenue. After that I asked about Willow and then Tower. They realized my questions coincided with the exit signs with those roads. I read the newspaper before I was three, and Dad drilled me on math. Every night, we put together a jigsaw puzzle of the United States with the state capitols listed under the pieces. The game was to name the capitol and remove the piece.

Long story short, the kindergarten, first, second, and third grade teachers in Lake Bluff had nothing to teach me. Bored as hell, I turned to comedy to pass the time, and I killed every day. Every once in a while I would stumble onto a piece of information that Mom and Dad failed to stuff into my brain, so I would briefly pay attention. Clever teachers would give me projects to complete while they taught the rest of the students to read, but my primary focus from 8:30 a.m.-3:15 p.m. every weekday from the day after Labor Day until June 15th was to make classmates laugh.

My thirst for laughs was boundless, and there was no level of shame I would refuse to endure in order to earn laughter. Teachers were powerless to stop me. I got straight A's, so the failure was theirs. If teachers couldn't find a way to keep my mind occupied, that was their problem — or so I saw it.

My record against elementary school teachers was 6-1. Four retired, one was promoted, and the sixth became a San Diego house painter. The only teacher against whom I was not victorious was Mrs. Anderson. She knew how to keep me busy in first grade. I assembled bookmarks from construction paper like it was my job. Mom would ask, "What did you do at school today?" I told her about the bookmarks every day for a week. She and my dad weren't happy about it, but short of changing the curriculum to suit my needs, what was Mrs. Anderson supposed to do?

The worst year was third grade. On registration day, we filed into the gym to see who our teachers would be. We also got a look at who else was in our class. It was clear Mrs. Gemmer would be facing a challenge. Her class roster was like the 1927 New York Yankees of malcontents, knuckleheads, and loudmouths. If Attention Deficit Disorder had existed back then, each of us would have been diagnosed and medicated. Back then, they called us "challenging" — and as a group the challenge was substantial.

Mrs. Gemmer was a little long in the tooth to connect with third graders, and she was strained to the point of making drunken phone calls to my parents at ten at night within the first month. We didn't do anything dangerous or obnoxious in class — just practiced ceaseless civil disobedience. October brought a visit from Mr. Lemerlee, our principal, at the end of a mischievous Wednesday. "In 14 years as a professional educator, I have never even heard of a class that behaved this badly. You are driving Mrs. Gemmer crazy," he said. The class proudly laughed. "This is nothing to be proud of!" Mr. Lemerlee scoffed as he left the room.

If anything, Lemerlee's visit sealed our zeal for classroom antics. One day, as Mrs. Gemmer was writing on the blackboard, the class turned our desks 180-degrees so they faced the window. Another time while Mrs. Gemmer had her back to us while helping a student at her desk, six of us snuck behind a partition. When Mrs. Gemmer stormed into the hallway to look for us, we silently ran back to our desks. She came back in, and hit the intercom button to report us to the office. Before the answer came, she noticed we were back. All of us had deadpan expressions as though we never left our seats. Mrs. Gemmer told the school secretary over the crackly speaker, "Never mind."

At the end of the semester, Mr. Lemerlee returned to our classroom to tell us the two third grade classes would be merged into one giant super class. We were elated, as though we had perpetrated some holy insurrection against authority.

The rest of the year was mostly uneventful, and Mrs. Gemmer quietly retired at the end of the year.

Our fourth grade teacher was Mrs. Georgevich. She was prone to anger in the face of revolt rather than Mrs. Gemmer's style of resignation, so we made an effort to comport with school norms. There might have been more trouble in fourth grade, but my innate reservoir of reading, math, and geography knowledge finally ran dry. I needed to pay attention in order to succeed.

Still, there was enough silliness that Mrs. Georgevich yelling, "Kent Sterling, what in the blue blazes are you up to now," still rings in my ears. She made me write sentences at least once a week. I still remember the sentence — "I am not only being unfair to my teacher and classmates, but also the taxpayers of Lake Bluff. I promise not to do this again." That's a pain in the ass for a fourth grader to write 25 times, but not a big enough pain for me to stop trying to amuse classmates. By the way, if I was being unfair to my classmates, why were they always laughing?

I've made it sound like I was an educational career — ender. For a couple of teachers, I was, but I got along exceptionally well with a few of them — those who were interesting, or more accurately, those who were interested in what they were teaching. The job of a teacher is not to present information, but to get students to stuff lessons somewhere in their brains. If no one remembers a lesson because a teacher was bored with it — what's the point?

Holding teachers accountable for their tedious performance was my game. There needs to be a consequence for indifferent instruction. I was that consequence.

In seventh grade, I had a great English teacher. Mrs. Cook allowed me to wander around a little bit during class, and when we were supposed to read quietly, I laid on the air conditioning vents. Mrs. Cook told my parents that she never allowed anyone else to do that. I was an exception because she trusted that if the principal popped into the classroom, I would hop into my desk before he ever saw me. She was right. I knew how not to get caught, and how to cover for co-conspirators.

Mrs. Cook was also a very good writing instructor for me. She always encouraged us to write what we knew, and what entertained us. I wrote about incidents with other teachers that illustrated why I did not respect them. Mrs. Cook must not have thought highly of them either because I got a lot of A's.

As I mentioned earlier, Attention Deficit Disorder did not exist as a diagnosis back in the 1970s, and there were certainly no pharmaceuticals to address its symptoms. We just muddled through as best we could as we clumsily communicated what we needed from teachers. I may have missed a couple of math lessons while I was otherwise occupied by my need to enteratain, but I wouldn't trade any of the life lessons I was exposed to for a deeper knowledge of fractions.

Lessons learned:

1. Embrace your uniqueness.

2. The school was built for the students, not the teachers.

3. School is about more than reading, writing, and arithmetic.

4. Life's too short to patiently wait to be interested.

Hey, Where's My Present?

Presents are good. I liked them when I was a kid. Hell, I like them now. Gifts offer the opportunity for hopes and wishes to be granted. Every box colorfully wrapped holds the promise of a dream come true.

My affinity for receiving as many presents as possible has dimmed over the years. Better put, I have embraced a philosophy where giving surprises to those I love and appreciate trumps the greed -fueled frenzy of my youth.

But when I was 12 I was the most enthusiastic recipient in the history of Christmas and birthdays. I always campaigned for the biggest possible birthday party. Several classmates at Lake Hills Elementary in Spring Lake, Michigan, had their birthday parties at the local roller rink. The entire grade was invited. For those keeping track, that meant 49 presents. What a magnificent buffet of toys and games those lucky birthday celebrants enjoyed.

My imagination was boggled by the sheer tonnage of presents. It probably took those kids an hour to open every gift, and a month could go by without having the opportunity to play with all of them.

My parents decided I should have a slumber party, which was cool, but meant a greatly reduced number of guests. Girls were eliminated immediately, which halved the potential bounty. I told Mom and Dad there were 24 boys in

22

the sixth grade. Where would they all sleep? They told me to invite six guys. That was an unacceptably small number of gifts compared to the roller rink magic. My God, that degree of reduction was silly. I tried to negotiate the number upward, but my parents held firm.

I settled on my five best friends, and all agreed to come. Jay, Jeff, Paul, Peter, and Tim arrived for the party, and we began playing games immediately. Dad brought out his enormous instant portrait camera for mugshots which he collected at every event in our lives. We played charades at he insistence of my mom. Tell me the last time you heard of a group of sixth graders playing charades at a birthday party. I'm not sure whether to be a proud iconoclast or a humiliated weirdo.

My birthday is February 22nd, so playing outside was impossible. There was constant snow cover from late November into mid March, and Mom and Dad were not about to have seven guys traipsing mud and snow around the house — not one week before we were moving back to Lake Bluff.

The demographic at my elementary school was quite broad from a socioeconomic perspective. There were sons and daughters of doctors, others who lived in a trailer park, and everyone else fell somewhere between.

I never paid any attention to whether people came from money or not. My currency was laughter. If a kid could make me laugh, that was enough for me. If he or she had a bit of a subversive soul, all the better.

Cake and ice cream were served, and it was finally time to open the presents. There were four of them, which I opened in a frenzy. As I finished, I did the math — five guests minus four gifts equaled one missing gift. Jay gave me a gift, and so did Jeff. Tim and Pete had also ponied up. That left Paul.

While I loved gifts at a level difficult to comprehend, I coveted the truth. That Paul did not bring a gift was disappointing, but I needed to know why. It did not seem Paul was going to volunteer the information, so I would have to ask him and hope he trusted me enough to tell me. I didn't want to embarrass him, but if I didn't ask, I would never know.

Bedtime came, and everyone went downstairs into the basement. Paul lagged behind a bit which gave me a great opportunity to speak to him privately. "Paul, I noticed you did not bring a gift. Is there a reason?" My honest —to — God intent in asking was to let him know it's OK that he didn't bring a gift. If Paul said money was tight or that because of his religious beliefs it was inappropriate, I would have been cool with that. The phrasing of my question was more like, "Hey dickhead, where's my damn present? What do you think birthday party means?"

Paul's response pleased me: "I forgot it. Sorry about that. I'll bring it to school Monday." That meant I would have a gift waiting for me on a day when there was nothing at all to look forward to otherwise. I went to bed happier than if Paul had brought a present to the party. This would be like a birthday version of Hanukkah. Pulsing presents across another day was a revelation. This was my best birthday ever!

Monday came, and with great excitement I met Paul's bus outside our classroom. His hands were empty, and I was flummoxed. Seeking the truth, I asked again about the twice overdue present. "Sorry, I forgot it again," he said. Through the day and night, I clung to the small hope that Paul would show up at school with the present the following day.

You have already figured out what it took me three interactions with Paul to figure out. He didn't have a present, and my need for yet another one was embarrassing. Thank God I had the decency to watch him get off the bus the next day through our classroom window instead of accosting him as he unboarded.

Trust has never been a problem for me. You tell me the sky is green — at the very least I look out the window. Paul was a good dude, and I shouldn't have cared about a gift. As this book testifies, I'm a reasonably willing participant in unearthing my mistakes and putting them in the brains of those who might judge me as a slow-to-process moron, but this episode with Paul has bothered me since it happened. Part of the reason might be that I moved away from Spring Lake three days after that Tuesday, and the other part would be that I was a selfish present-hungry ass.

Over the years, I've pieced together small bits of information and conversations that led me to believe Paul lived in the trailer park, and was part of a family that likely had very little disposable cash for goofy toys that might amuse a sixth grader.

Most mistakes are forgivable and the lessons learned easily outweigh the offending or ludicrous activity. This one I have a difficult time forgetting or forgiving.

Lessons learned:

1. Be happy for what you have — and share it.

2. Don't hold people accountable for gifts — their presence is their present.

3. Demanding total honesty and transparency is silly. Allow people to share truths within their comfort zone.

Fight! Fight! Fight!

When I was in elementary school, I liked to fight. Settling arguments was easy. The kid who won the fight won the argument. Back then, it wasn't even discouraged by teachers or parents. Then, on the last day of fourth grade Bill Arndt punched me in the ear — hard. I thought for two hours I was deaf. That cured me of fighting. Until seventh grade.

The migration to junior high launched a couple hundred 12-year-olds into an unpredictable social environment where frustration between wise-asses and brutes ended in violence. The guys who hit puberty early exerted physical dominance and those a little behind the maturity curve compensated through becoming clever. Brutes loved pummeling wise-asses, and wise-asses were powerless to resist the temptation to mock the brutes. I was a wise-ass and Matt Keller was a brute. It was inevitable we would square off eventually.

Keller was a reasonably nice guy most of the time, and not terrible big, but occasionally got physical. He would whack kids on the head with a pencil, thwack ears, kick the backs of knees, and visit other childish and dopey physical torment on other seventh graders unlikely to return fire. It was his only defense against those who easily outwitted him, and it was tolerated because physical mischief was his only weapon. Misery would be his soon enough when salaries were earned based upon intellect. We knew that even as 12-year-olds.

One day in fifth period study hall as we walked to a different classroom, Keller and four equally dull boobs began a mass hammering of my head with pencils of various thickness. Fighting all of them was too bold a move for a skinny guy like me, but I was capable of leaving school before I exploded in a self—indulgent and ultimately foolish rage. As the class took a right turn down the hall and the whacking continued, I bolted straight out the door and walked to my grandmother's place a few blocks away.

I explained what happened as my grandmother watched an episode of "Perry Mason." She offered me one of the Sau-Sea Shrimp Cocktails she always had in the refrigerator in case I came by. "You should call your father," she told me. That didn't happen very often. Dad and "May-May" saw eye to eye on very few topics, other than their shared love of family, so I picked up the phone and dialed.

Dad was not going to be happy I left school, but he would certainly see the wisdom of pacifism in the face of a threat of group violence against his borderline scrawny son. After all, I was not *The Outlaw Josey Wales* able to tame five pistoleros by having the sun at my back and nothing to lose. I would have been beaten senseless. Dad told me to wait at my grandmother's and he would be there in a couple of minutes to give me a lift back to school.

"Here's what you're going to do," Dad told me during the very short drive back to school. "The next time one of these idiots gets physical with you, hit him as hard as you can. I promise you that will be the last time any of them touch you." Dad was prone to loud outbursts, but he was almost solemn as he gave me my orders. "I'm going into the school with you, and I'm going to explain to Mr. Itzof what you did and what I've told you to do next time it happens."

This was a side of Dad we rarely saw. He had three emotional states — anger, laughter, and sleep. At least that's how I remember him. But he was also unfailingly loyal to his family. The more dire the situation, the quieter Dad became. He was built for turbulent times, and his greatest strength was wasted when waters around him were calm.

We walked straight into the office where Principal Itzof and Mr. Thompson, the study hall teacher, were talking about me. Dad didn't wait for a greeting. "Kent's back. He left because he saw no other solution to the pack of morons who were whacking him in the head. I told him the next time any boy touches him, he's to punch him as hard as he can. Because I told him this, he shouldn't be held accountable. If anyone is punished for what he does, it should be me because the consequence for him if he doesn't do what I told him will be worse than what you are allowed."

He turned to me and said, "Go back to class." Then he walked out. Neither Itzof nor Thompson said anything. They just looked at Dad with a combination of confusion, fear, and awe. This happened quite a bit. Dad never waited for a counterpoint to his argument. That guaranteed a win in his book.

Keller and the other whackers steered clear of me for a couple of weeks. Then during study hall, as I worked on a paper for sixth period English, Keller ran past my desk and grabbed my pen. He stood in the front of the classroom taunting me with the pen. It was time to put Dad's "throw hands first/ask questions later" tactic to the test.

I got up, walked up the aisle toward Keller. He grinned. I made a fist and threw it against his cheekbone as hard as I could. Momentarily stunned, Keller fell back five or six feet, and gathered his wits. His face went from stunned puzzlement to wild rage, and he lunged at me. Mr. Thompson stepped between us as I went in for more. He yelled at us to take our seats.

No one called the office. No one issued any punishment. And for the rest of my time in Lake Bluff, the big guys were very friendly.

Dad was right. When I established a boundary by using a physical consequence, I earned the respect of those who dealt with life through physical confrontation. Fighting is seen as counter to maintaining order in schools, but a right cross to the jaw is a very solid deterrent to bullying.

I am not an advocate for unchecked physical violence, but there is something to be said for a kid showing everyone that he will not be manhandled by a bigger kid who tries to assert dominance.

The era of dads demanding sons fight their way out of trouble with bullies seems to have ended, but there is an unintended consequence to the banishment of those who fight fire with fire. The bullies win by default, and the weak feel impotent as a result.

I learned a lot from my dad, and that car ride back to school followed by a very solid one-way 45-second conversation between he and the school principal taught me almost everything I needed to know about being a seventh grade boy — and a father.

Taking the fight to the bully works — then, today, always. I'm not advocating wanton violence in the halls or classrooms of our schools, but at the right place and time, the threat of violence backed up by an occasional and well-deserved punch can be a very solid deterrent to bullying.

Lessons learned:

1. Almost no one wants to get hit, and that fear stops 99% of potential fights before they start.
2. Bullies smell fear and reluctance to engage, so don't fear engagement.

3. Getting your ass kicked once beats the hell out of being tormented forever.

4. Listen to your father. He knows things you don't.

Candy, Baseball Cards, Dancing and Lessons at White's

White's Variety Store was the nexus point for children in Lake Bluff. Seemingly, every kid there blew his or her allowance each week at White's. Mr. White, (Lake Bluff was and is the kind of town where the owner is in the store) stocked the shelves with all the things kids loved — toys, candy, baseball cards, and bubble gum. He also had some adult items like extension cords, vases, greeting cards, and other boring stuff, but I never spent a second in those aisles.

My grandmother lived in an apartment on the second story of the building that housed White's, the laundromat, the A&P, and a dry cleaners. That made her exceptionally lucky in my book. Everyone else had to ride their bikes to White's but I only had to walk downstairs when we visited, which was often because Lake Bluff was a very small town. Her apartment was also the best place in town to watch the Fourth of July Parade.

Kids met at White's, shopped at White's, dreamed at White's, and stole at White's. Yes, I stole from White's — twice. I'll get to that later. Kids also asked each other out on dates at White's — at least I did, once.

The first and only time I asked a girl to a junior high dance was in front of White's. I rode my bike to my grandmother's apartment after school one day in eighth grade, and I told myself that if Marj was at White's, I would ask her to Friday's dance. Incredibly, Marj's bike was parked out front — back then kids were known by the make, model, and color of their bikes just as adults with cars. We all knew what everyone else rode. As she exited the store, I asked "Would you like to go to the dance?" She said yes with a sweet smile.

I was euphoric as I rode home because I had never asked a girl to do anything before. The potential for rejection was just too terrifying. But Marj said yes! After telling my mom that I had a date to the dance, she asked *the* question: "What does that mean?" She went on to ask more specific questions, like, "Are you supposed to pay for her? Should we pick Marj up? Will you dance together?" Holy crap! I hadn't considered any of this minutiae before I asked Marj to go to the dance. The odds of her being at White's were not good, and I hadn't thought anything through.

Marj was a cute girl who could make me laugh. She was sweetly funny — kind of like a 14-year-old Carol Burnett. Laughter was a big deal with me. I respected funny people much as others prize work ethic or intellect. She wore her hair in one of two ways — either with ponytails or braided pigtails. I liked the devil-may-care non-braided pigtails. Everyday in Mr. Hastings science class, I would wait for Marj to pass by to see which she had chosen that day. Whenever I saw the braids, I thought, "Doesn't she know the unbraided pigtails suit her personality so much better?"

The questions Mom asked were good ones, and Marj's mom might have been asking them too. Not wanting to appear as dopey as I knew I was, I never answered those questions for anyone. I showed up at the site of the dance, a church, alone having not said a word to Marj since she accepted my invitation. I hoped the brief interlude at White's made Marj as nervous as it made me.

I stood outside the church in the middle of six friends as we waited for the doors to open. Marj was 20 feet away in the middle of her friends, and I positioned myself carefully to make sure she couldn't see me. She kept scanning the crowd, and I kept ducking. Finally, Nick shifted unexpectedly, and I was exposed. Marj walked over, "Here I am!" I said something lame, and in we went. Bamboozled by whether I should pay for Marj, I paid only for me. My thinking at the time was that if I wasn't supposed to pay but did, I would be out a buck. If I didn't pay, but was supposed to, I would still have the back. My shameful rule at the time was, when in doubt hold onto your cash.

The band at this dance, and almost all of our dances, played nothing but Chicago covers, which was cool back then. There was one horrifying song that spooked my friends and me. "Colour My World" is a slow song that meant we had to hug girls while shuffling our feet. During "Colour My World" we sought refuge upstairs in the room with the bumper pool table. I spent a lot of time playing bumper pool at junior high dances because none of my classmates looked cool as they danced. They looked like buffoons, and I had an aversion to looking like a buffoon. It never occurred to me that everyone looks ridiculous when they dance if they don't dance with confidence or indifference. I was not indifferent — so I did not dance.

I wasted the entire dance avoiding Marj, or claiming to have a tremendous headache in our few conversations. In the moment, I felt like a jerk. It seemed smart at the time to restrict that knowledge to myself rather than admit my ignorance and embrace vulnerability. All these years later, I still feel like an idiot. Marj was a nice girl, and we could have had a fun night getting to know each other and had a couple of dances. I should have been out a dollar, and should have stopped by her house as I walked to the church.

And now for my shoplifting episode:

I stole twice from White's. When I was three, my parents left me there to amuse myself as they grabbed something quick at the A&P next door. That would be unthinkable today, but in a town like Lake Bluff in the 1960s, it was common for parents to leave kids for a few minutes as they played with toys in a store like White's. My toy of choice that day was a red fire truck, and when I noticed Mom and Dad were gone, I grabbed the truck and hoofed it to the A&P.

Mom and Dad weren't detectives, but they noticed the fire truck — almost as big as I was — I was carrying. They surmised I lifted it from White's and took me back there to return it. To a three-year-old, the idea of exchanging currency for goods is as foreign as seeing boobs as anything but a source of food. There was no lesson to learn as I didn't understand the offense.

No harm, no foul. Mr. White laughed as he returned the truck to the shelf.

It's different for an eight-year-old, so when I grabbed a single jawbreaker and put it in my pocket it was safe to assume I knew what I was doing. To this day, my face continues to expose all truths. I'm great to play poker with. When I feel joy, I appear joyous. When I am angry, I look angry. When I stole as an eight-year-old, I looked like an eight-year-old who had somebody else's jawbreaker in his pocket.

The cashier, a nice woman named Jane, called me back into the store and said, "Kent, what's in your pocket?" I pulled out the jawbreaker and put it on the counter. She said, "I'm very disappointed in you. I need to talk to your mom about this. What's your phone number?"

Now, I've never been good at hiding wrongdoing, but I'm no fool. I told her, "234-1023," which was my grandmother's number.

"Is she home now?" Jane asked. I told her she was, and walked quickly up the 20 stairs to my grandmother's apartment. Almost on cue, the phone rang and I answered.

"Hello?"

"Mrs. Sterling?"

"Yes."

"This is Jane at White's. I caught Kent stealing a penny jawbreaker a few minutes ago. No big deal — just thought this would give you a great chance to teach him a lesson."

"Well, thank you very much. Goodbye." That was that.

I must have sounded like my mom.

White's closed in 1982 because the new owners of the building raised the rent to the point where selling candy and toys to children no longer made economic sense for Mr. White. Lake Bluff moved on without the store where kids learned, laughed, and developed a taste for sweets. Mr. White passed away in 2010 at the age of 101. But the lessons and laughs remain with the kids who spent their allowances there.

Lessons learned:

1. Communicate, even if it means admitting ignorance. Some people find that charming.

2. Chicago cover bands should be outlawed. Come to think of it, I haven't heard one since that eighth grade dance.

3. Stealing is bad, but if you can keep your parents from finding out, that's a win.

4. Dancing poorly beats playing bumper pool well.

Four Fearless Months
Bring Out My Best

One day after I came home from school in eighth grade, Dad asked, "You want to be a congressman, right?" This was before I knew what a congressman needed to do to be elected and remain in office, and I thought it might be a noble pursuit. I told him I did. He said, "How would you like to be a congressman from Kentucky?"

That's how I found out we were moving from my idyllic childhood home in Lake Bluff to the Louisville area. It's hard to explain how beautiful Lake Bluff is. As you might guess, it's on the Lake Michigan shoreline, and there is a bluff that separates the town from the water.

I loved Lake Bluff in every way, and still do. There are 5,000 residents, and at the time it seemed like half of them were relatives and friends. Both of my grandmothers lived there, along with aunts, uncles, cousins, and almost everyone I had ever known. Forty years later, it's mostly unchanged, other than my relatives moving to other parts of the Midwest — just as we were about to.

I was not a great student. I was in honors classes, but had to apply myself to get Bs and Cs. Kids in Lake Bluff were smart — *really* smart. To give you an idea of the difference between Lake Bluff and New Albany, Indiana (the town to which we would move), I immediately became an honor student at New Albany and remained one for three years without listening to a teacher or opening a book until the second semester of my junior year.

Dad took a job as a manufacturer's rep for a business that specialized in heating and cooling, but because he was a great guy he decided to commute for three months to allow me to go on the eighth grade Washington D.C. trip with my Lake Bluff classmates. I had looked forward to that trip from the time I was in third grade, and Mom and Dad agreed that uprooting me so close to the journey would be cruel.

The day after Dad encouraged a geographical shift in my political ambitions, we started the school day with an assembly in the gym. Somebody was yammering about something, so I turned to Rodney Turpel, a friend of mine, and told him we would be moving after the Washington trip.

Rodney's eyes darted back and forth for several seconds. He smiled and said, "Do you know what that means?" I told him I didn't.

"You get to live life without consequence until April," Rodney told me. "Whatever happens between now and then, you get a clean slate when you move. If your grades suck, who cares? If you make an ass of yourself, who cares? You are playing the rest of eighth grade with house money!"

This was a revelation to me. I had not looked at the interval between moves as anything but a purgatory — a living wake where I would get to live my current life for a brief period before moving on to a new one.

I have always been fortunate in surrounding myself with people at least slightly smarter than I am, and Rodney's immediate reaction was an epiphany. Looking back at it now, I'm amazed how quickly he deduced how the move could benefit my short term future.

Before being awakened to the possibility of behavior without accountability, I had never considered the concept. I needed to fear nothing. Getting an F on a test was without meaning. Being looked down upon or mocked by very popular kids was no longer a terrible thought. I could tell people whatever popped into my mind, and in four months I would be a footnote in their lives, just as they would be in mine.

This kind of freedom from judgment can move a person in many directions. My choice was to embrace everything — to do whatever I wanted without fear or any self-imposed constraint.

I began treating popular kids and good-looking girls as equals, which baffled them at first. I started studying a little more because I wanted to learn rather than avoid grade-related failure. When a poster was hung in the halls announcing the audition for the junior high talent show, I signed up as a potential emcee.

This was exactly like when people say, "If you had months to live, what kind of person would you be?" I had four months to live as a resident of Lake Bluff and eighth grader at Lake Bluff Junior High, and I chose to be the best version of myself without fear of judgment.

In both seventh and eighth grade math class, I had a teacher named Mr. Johnson who had a poster board with all of our names listed vertically and all tests and assignments horizontally. Anyone who placed in the top five would get a star at the intersection of his or her name and the assignment or test. Gold was for 1st place, silver for 2nd, red for 3rd, green for 4th, and blue for fifth.

I might have eked out two blue stars during that first year an a half. But freed from my shackles of fear, all of a sudden math got really easy. Instead of studying out of duty and being scared of my parents' disappointment, I studied because I wanted to learn.

Stars cropped up with everything Mr. Johnson graded. All of a sudden, I was smart. It didn't make a hell of a lot of sense to me then. I thought it was bizarre — right when it no longer mattered if I got an F, I started hanging As.

Popular people started sitting near me and talking to me. I answered with sincerity and irreverence as an equal, and never held back anything. Instead of trying not to offend, I started communicating. I didn't trust their friendship at first. I believed they were just being nice to the guy who was moving, a geographically terminal kid. Then I adjusted and embraced the best case scenario, again, because there was no downside to trust being broken.

The talent show audition happened, and Rodney and I decided to try out as a duo. He was stout with round Italian features, and I was skinny and Irish. We were a little like a midwestern version of Laurel & Hardy.

We did no preparation at all. Just showed up and riffed. I didn't know what improvisation was then, but that's what we did. I imagine it was horrible, but we didn't care. It was fun, and at that point fun was all I was looking for.

Fortunately, there weren't many polished 14-year-old performers running around Lake Bluff, and we were cast as the emcees for half the show. Our job was to introduce singers, skits, and other odd pieces of staged buffoonery. We decided to expand our introductions to create moments of our own.

We showed up for rehearsals, and no introduction was the same twice. We decided to dress as and play the idiotic pitchmen for the now-defunct A&P chain of grocery stores. "Price" was a skinny guy and "Pride" was a little girthy, so we fit the profile.

The night of the show, we felt utterly unprepared because despite working hard in rehearsal, neither of us had ever performed before. We had one advantage — ambivalence to the response of dutiful parents and classmates who showed up out of obligation. If we were even a little funny, it would be a massive relief to everyone.

And we were more than a little funny. In three years of improvisation a decade and a half later, I never had a night like this. Rodney was hilarious. We played off each other effortlessly, and never broke character.

For the next six weeks, people treated me as the person I always believed myself to be. The irony of all this good stuff happening because of my "temp" status was not lost on me.

Had I never moved, I would likely have stayed the curious and weird C+ student who was funny in a pinch, but now I had to move and start from scratch as the guy who had become who he always should have been.

We moved. I was heartbroken, but infinitely wiser.

Lessons learned:

1. Live everyday as the best version of you without fear of judgment. To hell with what others think. Don't be a sociopath, but definitely embrace confidence, because in the end — why the hell not?

2. The worst sometimes brings the best, and the best sometimes ushers in the worst. Try not to take too seriously the good or the bad.

3. Never forget that what seemed bad in the moment may have prevented something miserable. Had we stayed in Lake Bluff, there is no guarantee my life would be better.

Can't Hit the Curve

I loved baseball growing up, and still love it. Everything about it was fun. Watching it, playing it, inventing mutations of it when we didn't have enough people to play a real game. Hell, I would stand in our side yard, throw tennis balls up and hit them into the trees all afternoon long when there wasn't another kid around to play catch with.

Baseball cards were bought and sorted by birthdate, height, career batting average, career home runs, and number of teams played for.

Christmas was a big day for me, but the best day of the year was when my dad pulled me out of school to go to Wrigley Field for a Cubs game. I never knew when it was coming, so every day the Cubs played at home (all home games started at 1:20 p.m. back in the 1970s) I hoped he would roll up and grab me during lunch.

When I was 10, I signed up for a twice per week summer baseball camp. Workouts started at nine in the morning. If it rained the night before, I got there at eight with a rake. Puddles on the infield were grounds for cancelling camp that day, so I raked my ass off to make sure there were no puddles. The counselors were disappointed several times by what seemed to be miraculous drainage on the diamond.

One day at camp, we were shagging fly balls. I always caught fly balls one handed. Seemed odd to use a second hand to me, and I had never dropped one, so I stuck with what made sense. Coach Hansen stopped hitting fly balls after I caught several. He used me as an example as to how not to catch a fly ball, and being the arrogant little prick I was, I told him, "I don't need to use two hands. You can hit me 1,000 flies, and I won't drop any."

Hansen looked at me with patient disdain, "Sterling, if catching fly balls with one hand works as well as two, why does every outfielder in the majors use two?"

With all the hubris a 10-year-old can exhibit, I replied, "They don't. Willie Mays and Rico Carty use one hand. Jerry Morales too."

Hansen lowered his head, walked back to the plate, and continued to hit flies. And I continued to catch them one-handed.

In the field, I was supremely confident. At the plate, I was a terrified mess. Hitting meant standing inches from where a hard projectile was hurled.

I got hit once. Only once. But the lesson stuck. I was nine years old, and a kid named Johnny Palmer was pitching. For a kid that age, Johnny threw pretty hard, and he caught me in the funny bone with a pitch. As physiology demands, the nerve being concussed caused my left pinky and the left half of my ring finger to go immediately numb. Fear that I was permanently damaged caused me to melt as I got to first base. I didn't cry because on some level I didn't want to admit it was a big deal, but I was terrified my left pinky had been rendered useless.

From that point forward, my primary purpose at the plate was to avoid getting hit. Dad would yell, "Stop dancing up there!" I would ignore him. He would tell me the best thing that could happen to me would be to get hit again because I would realize it doesn't really hurt. I knew he was probably right because he was right most of the time, but I hedged my bets by continuing to avoid getting hit.

When I played Babe Ruth League baseball at age 15, Dad brought his boss to a game one night. I walked to the plate, began moving my feet like all I wanted in the world was to end the at-bat before taking one in the ribs, ass, or, God forbid, in the funny bone again.

Playing against 15-year-olds raised the stakes a little bit as pitchers were now throwing 80 miles per hour instead of 60, and this night a kid named Les Nemchek was pitching. He threw hard. First pitch was a strike, and I swung late and weakly without purpose. Dad had enough, and yelled, "Stand in there and hit the goddamned ball!" I stepped out of the box, and thought — okay, the old man has yelled at me in front of his boss. If I came with the same weak swing, it would make it seem like I didn't respect him, so I decided to nut up.

The next pitch was a fastball right down main street, because why the hell not? The first swing showed I wasn't there to hit, so Nemchek grooved one. I kept my right foot planted, strode toward the pitch, opened my hips, and dropped the barrel of the bat on the ball. The ball screamed into center field for a clean base hit.

This story would be the basis for its own book if I was smart enough to commit to the same attitude each time I came to the plate from that day until I finally got to the major leagues.

Instead of using this as a magical pivot point toward more aggressive quality at-bats, on my way to first I thought, "Well, there you go. I faced my demons once to allow you to appear to be a dad who had the ear of his son, but that's it! Never again." Yep, a split second after overcoming fear and seeing a positive result, I re-embraced it.

Even though I deeply loved the game — and still do — my ability to play despite an almost pathological aversion to hitting (or being hit) came to a head a couple of weeks later when I faced the great Denny Ferguson. He had a wicked breaking ball. I had never seen a good curveball until I saw three in succession against Denny.

The first one started right at my eyes. I bailed. Hit the dirt. Took refuge on my ass. The umpire called strike one. I looked at him like he was nuts. He quietly repeated, "Strike one," and grinned. Second pitch started — again — right at my eyes. Hit the dirt — again. He barked "Strike two!" with a bigger grin. Guess what happened with the third pitch? Yep, big hook that started at my eyes — again. "Strike three!" shouted the ump with a cackle.

Walking back to the dugout I was mystified. Our manager Mr. Cotner shook his head, "Three curveballs. He's pretty good. Shake it off." There was no shaking off a humiliating experience like being called out on three pitches while I sat petrified in the dirt. That night I knew it. No matter how much fun it was shagging flies and throwing guys out, there was just no way I was going to go through the misery of learning how not to flinch when Denny started curveballs at my brain.

In this battle of fight or flight, I chose to fly. Baseball was over for me.

Pathetic, right? Not a proud chapter of my life. Not being willing to overcome my fear of the ball pushed me to never allow that to happen again.

I might feel fear, but I'll never again allow it to rob of me something I love.

Lessons learned:

1. In the batter's box and life — plant your feet and attack!

2. Always listen to your father, not just when his boss is around.

3. Whatever your love is, find a way over, through, or around your fears to continue to indulge it.

4. Baseballs really don't hurt much until they're traveling better than 90 miles an hour, and even if one conks you in the noodle, you're wearing a helmet, so get over yourself and swing the damn bat!

Hey Now, You're an All-Star, Get Your Game On, GO PLAY!

The first question a teacher asked me after I moved to New Albany was, "Do you think New Albany can beat Jeff in the sectional next year?" I had no idea what any part of that question meant. Basketball in suburban Chicago was not a priority for sports fans in the late 1970s. In southern Indiana, basketball was — and is — everything

In Lake Bluff, tennis was top dog. We played tennis every day when weather allowed. Guys actually passed on playing travel baseball to play for the tennis team. Baseball was second in popularity. Football and soccer were third and fourth. Golf and hockey jockeyed for fifth and sixth. Basketball was a solid seventh. We played basketball, but not often and not well.

I was on the seventh grade basketball team, but rarely played. The team was terrible. We weren't bad athletes, but shooting around in a neighbor's driveway didn't prepare us to compete. The coaches had no idea what they were doing, so practices were not productive at all. That was cool because I had no interest in playing in front of 35 fans at Lake Forest High School. Soccer, tennis, golf, and track were more interesting to me than basketball.

In New Albany, the top five most popular sports were basketball, basketball, basketball, basketball, and basketball. It's still that way. Instead of the 35 parents and girlfriends watching the Scouts of Lake Forest, more than 4,000 routinely show up to cheer for the Bulldogs. In the movie *Hoosiers*, Gene Hackman's character says, "I thought everyone in Indiana plays basketball." He was right. Everyone plays and everyone watches. At least it feels that way.

Despite playing a lot of basketball after our move to New Albany, I never developed much of a feel for the game. I was just shy of six0feet tall in high school, so there was no chance whatsoever that I could play JV basketball, let alone varsity. I played soccer and golf in high school, and if not for the tennis season conflicting with soccer, I could have been the No. 2 player on our high school team. Hell, the top 20 players in my grade in Lake Bluff could have played No. 2 at New Albany.

My mediocrity didn't keep me from trying to enjoy basketball, so we put together an intramural team. I can't remember whether the organizers decided we should be the Trailblazers or if we named ourselves, but we had as much in common with the NBA's Portland franchise as a bottle of French's Mustard has with the Eiffel Tower.

What we lacked in dexterity and talent, we made up for with showmanship and clumsiness. Before every game we would warm up with an embarrassing homage to the Harlem Globetrotters' magic circle. In the first game, I fouled out before the end of the first quarter. The game ended early when Lewie Stevens used Tony Atkins' back as a step stool toward a dunk. Tony got down on all fours and Lewie leaped for what we thought was a highly entertaining bucket late in a blowout loss. The ref waved his arms and disqualified us while we celebrated like idiots.

Our senior year, New Albany had an extreme case of basketball fever as the high school team maintained an undefeated record all the way until the state championship game in Indianapolis. The five starters were 6'1", 6'9", 6'5",

6'8", and 6'8". Our intramural team may not have had a single player over 6'1", but that didn't keep us from enjoying ourselves on the court in one way or another.

Mr. Keeler ran intramurals, and he decided there should be an all-star basketball game played during homeroom in front of the student body. Students would be allowed to vote for the all-stars of their choice, and juniors would play the seniors. I was nothing if not fascinated by doing things in front of as many people as possible, so I initiated an aggressive campaign to land myself a position on the team.

I stood outside of Mr. Keeler's classroom and steered people toward the ballot box to vote for me. No one ever mentioned the vote totals, but I cannot imagine anyone outpolled me. No one invested any emotion or interest in this election but me, so despite being a borderline inept player, I was named a starter for the seniors.

As was often the case in high school, I rarely assessed the consequence of my actions, and far too often what seemed like a great idea in theory turned into a bit of a nightmare in reality. I had never played basketball in front of more than 100 people when I was a seventh grader, so nearly 1,500 people in New Albany's gym was intimidating.

I gave some thought to going full blown idiot to avoid the embarrassment of looking as bad at the game as I was. Being bad on purpose might be less humiliating than being bad because I genuinely sucked. During warmups, pride got the best of me, and I decided to play it straight to see if I could hang with a group that might have been the second best high school team in the Hoosier Hills Conference — behind only New Albany's varsity team.

The thing I noticed immediately was the athleticism of my teammates. They were all African-Americans who could play and jump and do all the other things basketball requires.

I knew enough about basketball to camp on the weak side to avoid the ball, and I was athletic enough to stay in front of my man on the defensive end. How bad could this be?

Have you ever noticed how, either in a book or conversation, the phrase, *How bad could this be,* is followed by a very good answer to that question?

My plan to avoid the ball was corrupted by two realities — because of my soccer conditioning, I was in exceptional physical shape and could run all day. And this game was nothing more than a series of fast breaks. I got out ahead of the ball on the first possession of the game and a kid named William Tutt appeared to prepare to pass the ball to his left. That was great because I was on the right. I'm not sure what happened, but the next thing I knew I was feeling my nose to see if it was broken. Apparently, William had faked left and thrown a no-look pass at my head. I thought briefly a wayward elbow might have caught me and a foul might be called. I looked at the ref and he laughed, saying "The ball hit you in the face!"

The next offensive possession, William missed a shot from the foul line and I got in position for the rebound. The ball came straight back off the rim to William, who batted the ball directly at my forehead. I never saw it coming, so it crashed against my skull with a loud thud. Unsure whether I was concussed, I hustled back on defense where the juniors turned the ball over again.

William ran the point of our three-on-two break, and passed early to the left. I was on the right, knifing toward the basket, ready to congratulate my teammate on a nice bucket. Sadly and predictably, that teammate was feeling generous and fired a pass to me rather than dunking the ball. The ball hit me in my left ear, and caused a severe ringing. The ball careened out of bounds, and Mr. Keeler subbed somebody in for me.

I wobbled toward the bench feeling like a sparring partner after a long day in the ring. I sat and gathered my faculties.

Midway through the fourth quarter, my head cleared and I was ready for more humiliation. I decided not to wait for Mr. Keeler to sub me back into the game. I reported to the scorer's table of my own volition, certain that Mr. Keeler had no authority to mete out meaningful punishment for my behavior during a silly homeroom activity. My only goal during the last three minutes was to avoid all contact with the ball. That was not a problem as it became obvious my teammates had no confidence in my ability to do anything other than let the ball crash into my skull, nose, or ear.

I don't remember whether we won or lost the game, and neither does anyone else. What they remember is their laughter at my expense — like I was the Jim Carrey of basketball, if Carrey was unintentionally funny. That afternoon in a variety of classes and in the halls, at least 50 people asked if I was OK. They did it while choking back laughter.

Lessons learned:

1. Stay in your lane.

2. If you have to campaign for your spot on a team, you will pay a price for inclusion.

3. Poor basketball players should stay behind the play.

4. If you suck, don't do it in front of more than 1,000 people — or 10 — or 1. Hell, do it alone.

Chemistry Class for Idiots — Or One Idiot

On the last day before my final exam for high school chemistry, Mr. Smith hosted a review session. He asked if anyone had a question. Because it might boost my attitude grade, I raised my hand.

"Yes, Kent, *You* have a question?" Mr. Smith was incredulous. I had never asked a question in his class. In fact, not once had I shown any interest.

I asked my question — something about valence, molarity, or some other elementary aspect of the stuff he had been teaching us for the past nine months. Mr. Smith responded without answering, "Good question. You come up with that while you were studying last night?"

"Yes, I did, Mr. Smith," I answered with a confident grin. Mr. Smith had never thrown any praise my way in that year in his class, and he was about to really not praise me.

"How'd you study last night without a book? Your textbook has been on my desk since January," Mr. Smith said with a sneer. "I'm really going to enjoy grading your final."

What Mr. Smith didn't know as he gleefully awaited what he believed to be impending doom for my academic future was that my eighth grade science teacher was a madman. Mr. Hastings was old school — *really* old school. He demanded that each of his students packed a year of both

51

college level chemistry and physics into their brains during that single year.

Mr. Hastings had no patience for foolishness, and even less for stupidity. He was a bald 6'2" World War II veteran with a right arm that bent oddly at the elbow. He always wore a white short sleeved dress shirt, a narrow tie, slacks, and the kind of old school square framed glasses Ohio State football coach Woody Hayes rocked. If you cast "A Christmas Carol" with junior high teachers, Mr. Hastings would have been Jacob Marley's ghost. He scared the hell out of students, teachers, and everyone else at Lake Bluff Junior High School.

Each year parents rained down complaints to the principal and school board about Mr. Hastings because their sons and daughters got C's and D's until they figured out how to work hard enough to succeed. No one complained after taking science from Mr. Hastings because somehow the lessons stuck. I still know the atomic weights of most of the elements in the periodic table and can tell you that the six noble gases are Helium, Neon, Argon, Krypton, Xenon, and Radon.

My command of basic chemistry has never revealed any use during my adult life, but the facts sit there fearing Mr. Hastings will one day show up most unexpectedly (as he has passed on) to quiz me on Avogadro's Number or ask that I solve an equation.

The hardcore teacher is now extinct because school administrators eventually tired of parent complaints about dictatorial and unforgiving taskmasters who forced kids to apply themselves. Mr. Hastings was one of those teachers that third graders heard about from eighth graders. "You better hope you never get Hastings," they would say. "He's demented. He teaches college chemistry and physics, and it's impossible!"

I worked my ass off in Mr. Hastings' class to get a low B. Looking back, I wish I had 50 Mr. Hastings as teachers.

My lack of focus in Mr. Smith's class did not mean I knew nothing about chemistry, and his little challenge in front of the rest of the class brought a little focus back to the undisciplined mush between my 17-year-old ears.

I showed up for the final with enthusiasm. Mr. Smith had made it a point to tell us the previous day that the final would be a standardized version "from the national office," whatever the hell that meant.

In fact, the standardized version was eerily similar to what I endured as an eighth grader. I flew through that 50-question multiple choice embarrassment in 20 minutes. When I handed it in, Mr. Smith grinned. I grinned back.

Mr. Smith was so eager to see the carnage my intellectual lethargy had wrought that he already had his red pen in hand by the time I reached his desk. He laid the key over my test, and his grin evaporated quickly. That red pen sat idle in Mr. Smith's right hand for extended periods as it made only three X's. For those of you keeping score at home, that's 47 correct answers for a score of 94%. Yep, the kid aced the big bad national office test, and the C-minus I took into the final morphed into a solid B right before the very disappointed eyes of Mr. Smith.

The lesson here is that focusing on learning regardless of the ability or desire of the teacher is something you owe yourself. It takes discipline to learn in spite of a teacher's indifference to his or her own lessons, but it's worth doing.

It took me awhile to develop some angst for Mr. Smith, but I have. I'm still not sure what kind of teacher allows a textbook to remain on his desk for four months while a kid soldiers on without it. I knew my book was gone, but thought I had misplaced it, or it had been stolen. All Mr. Smith had to do was give it back to me in January — as any reasonable educator should have done.

But then I couldn't have ruined his day with a little Mr. Hastings-instilled excellence.

Bolstered by my success in high school chemistry, I decided to accept an easy A for taking tests at Indiana University. The rules governing ions and neutrons hadn't changed, so I enrolled in an entry level chem class the second semester of my sophomore year.

There was a choice between two chemistry classes. C101 was elementary chemistry, but my eye went to C100, which was one less than C101. I didn't know what that meant, but it had to be easier because it was 100 instead of 101. That's the kind of logic I used when selecting classes at IU, and it was the primary reason for my academic struggles.

I picked up a syllabus on the first day of class and bolted. One of the guys who lived on my dorm floor was also in the class, so I had a backstop in case things got squirrelly and the professor changed the schedule. My plan was to return for the first test and not a minute before — after all, I was one of Mr. Hastings' students. He taught me everything, so what was there to fear?

College was an exercise in time management. If I could get a B without working, what the hell was the point of investing hours and hours to improve it to a B+ or A-? I was serious about journalism as a major, and worked hard at it, but it seemed silly to blow a Friday night — or Thursday afternoon — studying for a required course in which I had neither interest nor acumen. This, admittedly, is a terrible attitude to have toward college, and if my son had aped that philosophy, my head would have exploded and the checks for tuition would have stopped.

I attended every class that semester except C100, but I never darkened the doorstep of that classroom until the first test six weeks into the semester.

I strode into the room full of myself, and sat next to my friend Pat in case he needed a little help. Pat seemed smart, but he was a freshman and might be in over his head.

The tests were distributed. I looked at the first question, and I almost lost consciousness. "Detail the chemical process that results in the fermentation of beer."

What the sweet hell was that? Fermentation of beer? Where was all the nuts and bolts stuff Mr. Hastings taught me? I looked at the blackboard, and right next to C100 was the answer to my concern, "Practical Applications of Chemistry."

I looked over the rest of the 10 questions and they were all similar. "What causes acid rain?" "How does gasoline propel a car?" I had no idea how to even begin to formulate a coherent response. Panicked, I decided to rely on Pat's knowledge gleaned through rigorous attendance — or at least more rigorous than mine.

I have never been a skilled cheat or liar. Maybe that's a good thing, maybe not, but I have always had a face that revealed what was going on in my head. If I lied, people looked at me in a way I knew the jig was up.

And, cheating always seemed a surrender to an educational system I felt I should be able to outwit. It was shameful to even consider cheating, but my synapses were firing in a unique sequence that tolerated corruption as an escape from the consequence my irresponsibility had wrought.

I copied Pat's answer about beer almost verbatim, but tanked the second answer. The professor seemed to be eyeballing the class with enthusiasm, so hedging my bet seemed wise. My thinking was quickly adapting to my new standing as an unrepentant cheat.

Pat's answers appeared to come from a sound grasp of the material, so I assumed his score would be in the A - to - B range, which meant for me to pass, I could afford to whiff on only three questions. I would have to hope that I copied the answers that Pat aced. I also tried to gain an understanding of the question through reading Pat's answer and then re-stating it in my own words.

The whole process was exhausting — trying to time my gaze at Pat's work when the professor's attention was fixed elsewhere. This was complicated as Pat flipped to the next page quickly after he answered the last question on each.

My most coy piece of trickery was flying through a nonsensical answer to the final question, so I would be able to turn in my test prior to Pat — the logic being if I finished before Pat, it was unlikely I was copying his work.

When I turned in the test, I gave the professor a confident smile and thumbs up. He took the test and placed it separate from the others, which I thought strange. That moment nested in my brain for the rest of the day. I couldn't get the image to leave my mind. Getting caught for cheating was abhorrent to me — even more than the actual act.

I awakened the next morning, a Saturday, and I just couldn't take it. A confident cheat would be able to put that moment out of his head, and prepare his performance in case he was confronted. I needed closure — immediate closure — so I looked up the professor's phone number and called.

"Hi, my name is Kent Sterling, and I'm a student in your C100 class. Yesterday, when I turned in my test, you separated it from the others, and it seemed odd to me," I said with all the confidence of a soon —to —be condemned man. "Why would you do that?"

"I thought you cheated, but I compared your work with those who sat near you, and none were similar," he said.

"Cheated! Really? Wow. Okay then. Have a great weekend," I said and then hung up. I was momentarily relieved, but then realized if my test didn't resemble anyone else's, my grade likely sucked. When I got the test back, I saw the C- and finally exhaled.

A man's gotta know his limitations, and mine keep me as honest as I can be. I am an atrocious poker player as my face lights up like a pinball machine when I have cards, and looks as though I'm in mourning when I don't. Can't help it.

The only negative thing about it is that I'm not sure whether I'm honest because my character demands it, or whether it's because I understand the practical fruitlessness of any attempt at deception. In the end, I suppose it doesn't matter. Honest is as honest does.

Lessons learned:

1. Studying hard in eighth grade pays off like a well invested 401K.

2. A little advance scouting of the classes you plan to take pays off.

3. Hard work beats cheating.

4. If it takes shoving it to a teacher to become motivated, that's fine. Whatever revs your engine works.

So You Want to be a Rock 'n' Roll Star

This is the story of fame briefly sought by five high school friends who wanted nothing more than to stand on stage and be treated like The Beatles for a few minutes. Gifted with a sense of the absurd, a penchant for self-promotion, and a heaping pile of youthful stupidity, this band not only never reached its potential, it ceased to exist before discovering whether it had any.

The idea was to form a band, fill our high school auditorium, make vaguely musical loud noises, and find out what it is like to be on stage. We didn't know any songs, and I'm not sure any of us actually played a musical instrument at the time. There were dozens of reasons our little initiative couldn't, shouldn't, or wouldn't work, and only one that it would — we refused to tell ourselves no.

We didn't have instruments, knowledge of how bands function to play a song in an 850-seat auditorium, or a name for the band. At a meeting, we decided to answer the easy questions first, and the easiest question was "What will we call ourselves?" Because we were taking Chemistry at the time, someone mentioned uranium, then uranium-238, and then we finally settled on uranium-235 because it's the radioactive isotope of uranium. If you have a choice, why not go radioactive?

We didn't have a drummer, so we didn't have drums. Drums seemed like a bit of a waste because we had seen plenty of teenage bands and no one played worth a damn, so why even screw around with something that would make us sound like hacks? We needed two guitars playing power chords, and loud rage-filled vocals. That's U235 rock 'n' roll, we decided.

Despite not wanting drums or a drummer, there was a theatrical aspect we liked to a guy in the back of the stage banging on things. Without a drum kit, we decided to build something from household crap that would at least look interesting. Steve would sit on top of an eight-foot step ladder we would put on a riser. Garbage can lids would be hung by ropes from two 2 X 4s wedged into the step ladder, and Steve would hammer them with wooden spoons. That satisfied our idiotic notion of what we should look like without screwing up the sound.

John and Chris would play guitar. I can't remember whether they knew how to play a little or volunteered to learn, but we knew where we could lay our hands on a couple of electric guitars and two amps, so there was no need to invest in equipment there.

Lewie and I would sing — or scream. Neither of us were in choir, but we felt comfortable taking a simple rock song and turning it into an angry anthem.

As for a bass, my recollection is that none of us knew one was necessary.

The key was finding the right song. "Wild Thing" by The Troggs had been remade by Jimi Hendrix in a way we liked, so it was both a hip choice and maybe the easiest guitar song ever written. The chords were simple — A, D, E, and G in different orders throughout. Hell, I could have played that.

We signed up for our high school talent show without auditioning, and decided rehearsing was a waste of time.

Each of us gathered props — Steve cut a Hawaiian shirt at the shoulders, drew a tattoo on his arm, and wore a Japanese Coolie hat. Lewie had a fedora, small sports coat, and tie. I grabbed a ratty shoulder length wig my mom bought in the 1960s and an acoustic guitar she bought at a garage sale for $5 that I could smash like Pete Townshend if the mood struck me.

John and Chris learned the song, and we felt great before being introduced. At the very least, we could reduce the music to chaos, stomp around, and claim victory as a band that had no business being a band in the first place.

Right before we went on, a friend named Mike asked what I was going to do with the guitar that was slung across my back like Bob Dylan walking to a gig in Greenwich Village in 1962. I told him I was going to destroy it. He said, "Here's a pro tip — loosen the strings. If you break a guitar with tight strings, they might snap and hit you in the eye."

That seemed like reasonable guidance. I loosened the strings while wondering where Mike had learned the intricacies of guitar breakage.

We went onstage to a raucous welcome of friends and classmates. John and Chris hit simultaneous A chords, and off we went. There was only one microphone on a stand, so Lewie and I shared like Bruce Springsteen and Steve Van Zandt, which I liked because it looked cool. I snuck a look back at Steve, and he looked great despite the ladder, spoons and lids as he made no noise. People were on their feet — not because of the quality of the music, but maybe a combination of our energy and the outrageousness of the spectacle.

"Wild thing! You make my heart sing!" we shouted as loud and pitch perfect as we could.

During what passed for a dual impromptu guitar solo, I laid waste to my mom's acoustic guitar in a whirling and violent frenzy that Townshend would have thought too angry and over the top. Shards of wood flew everywhere, and I was pleased Mike told me to loosen the strings. No point in losing an eye just to look cool.

We took our bows as the last chords echoed. Our four minutes in the spotlight was a success — how could it not be? Failure wasn't a possibility because we sucked, knew it, accepted it, and presented ourselves with the unbridled confidence and energy of five guys with nothing to lose.

Immediately after the show, we decided a second show was in order. That was too much fun not to do again.

We needed a faculty sponsor to take over the auditorium during homeroom, so we spoke to our radio teacher, Lee Kelley, who agreed as long as we raised money to defray the expense of the radio department's New York trip. That was cool by me as I would be on the trip, and whatever cost my parents less money, I was all about.

This show would be bigger, better, and more audacious. We decided to add another song. Cheap Trick had a hit with an old Fats Domino classic "Ain't that a Shame," and that fit our needs. The guitar chords were simple again — A, E, D, E7, and A7 — and we already knew the words — again.

A guy named Matt had some marketing ideas that included tee-shirts and posters. Matt might have mentioned other things, but he had us at tee-shirts and posters. He took pictures of us in costumes that defied logic. Lewie held a trumpet, clarinet, and bongos. I had a trombone. Chris wore mittens while holding his guitar. John wore headphones over a trucker's hat and held a stick mic. Steve posed with a toy version of an assault rifle. I had the jack from John's headphones in my mouth. None of it made any sense.

Matt decided our show should have fog and flash pods. We loved that. The more, the better. The tee-shirts and posters were delivered. Matt sold the tees and hung the posters. They looked weird in a great way. Lewie was a little peeved that I was listed on the posters as the lead singer. When he asked me about it, I told him, "You're listed as 'vocals and bongos,' and I was just 'vocals,' so I told Matt I should be 'lead vocals.' Even at this ridiculous level, bandmates quibble about billing!

Because I had already wasted mom's guitar, we needed something to destroy. Steve worked at a neighborhood grocery store, so we decided he should grab as many wooden produce crates as he could. We painted them black, and planned to stack them on the stage like Marshall amps.

For two weeks prior to the show I promoted it during morning announcements, touting U-235's most recent successful tour of the Inner Part of Outer Mongolia, whatever the hell that meant. The show quickly sold out, and the music was ready, because you can't screw up "Wild Thing" and "Ain't that a Shame." We even rehearsed the night before to get the levels just right.

We had some openers — like a couple of teachers who looked a little like The Blues Brothers. They lip-synched "Soul Man." Then it was our turn. The stage had been set early, just like the real concerts we saw at Freedom Hall in Louisville. The crates looked like speakers, and Steve's ladder and garbage can lid rig was lit by strobes.

I was briefly distracted when I looked out from the wings and saw my parents sitting in the front row. They had not mentioned their intent to attend, and I thought they might have difficulty understanding just what the hell was happening. I shrugged. If they wanted to see this debacle, that was on them. I was not going to temper any of our nonsense. The show, however juvenile and insipid, must go on.

We had John's brother Kevin introduce us. He wore a London Fog trench coat, and identified himself as being from the King Biscuit Flower Hour. When Kevin said, "Please welcome Uranium 235!" The noise was deafening. I couldn't hear a thing. John and Chris hit their first chords and Lewie and I started singing. We had no monitors. Who thought we would need them to hear ourselves over screams?

The noise never waned over our two songs. The screaming was relentless. We tried to keep ourselves close to the same spot in the song, but there was no point because no one could hear us anyway.

I smashed the produce crates/speakers with a baseball bat I grabbed backstage, and as I came back to the mic I noticed both flash pods had tipped over, spilling the powder that would cause flames to ignite under the curtain. I'm no prop master, but I was fairly sure that if they were activated, the auditorium would ignite. I ran over to Matt and told him not to press the button. As great a story as the show ending in flames might have been, I had no interest in carrying our charade that far.

The show ended, the screaming quieted, and then the fog rolled from the machine. Somehow, even the effects knew they were unnecessary given the showmanship and musical expertise of Uranium 235!

The experience of being in the middle of those two shows was a cross between being a member of Spinal Tap and being a Beatle. It was exhilarating, but a little strange as we had not earned any level of adulation through mastery of an instrument or songwriting. We were idiots with a dream that briefly came true.

Interestingly, Chris, John, and Lewie have become adept musicians, and given a reasonable facsimile of a drummer (no offense to Steve and his wooden spoons), we could actually have done something as a band.

I like to think this experience was perfect in its weirdness. Uranium-235 was a little thrill ride that was as much comedy as music. Hunter Thompson said, "Buy the ticket, take the ride." The ride lasted nine minutes, and that seemed right at the time. It still seems right.

Lessons learned:

1. Don't let ignorance stop you from doing something cool.

2. You don't need to be great at something to enjoy it.

3. The quality of the idea is more important than the precision of the execution.

4. When in doubt, smash a guitar.

5. There is always an appropriate Hunter Thompson quote — *always*.

Everything fell right for New Albany High School's basketball team in 1980. They went undefeated in the regular

Painting Providence

season, were ranked No. 1 in the state of Indiana, and the Jeffersonville Sectional became the New Albany Sectional when the gym at Jeff flooded during a storm.

New Albany was electric with anticipation for the sectional during a normal year, but this was something entirely different, especially for hormonal students who were bouncing off the walls on a quiet day.

High school basketball is the most important sport in southern Indiana. The film *Hoosiers* accurately portrays how much people care about a bunch of high school kids throwing a leather ball through a hoop. Adults know everyone on the team, can recite their stats, and have scouted the junior highs to project what the team might be like in four or five years.

Sectional week is a huge event at New Albany, where some students stay in school until 10 or 11 p.m. to decorate the halls as a representation of their enthusiasm. Six hours of school followed by seven hours of painting and hanging signs can lead to questionable decisions, and so it was during my senior year as we got ready to play Providence High School in the sectional semifinals.

Boredom crept into my mind on Tuesday night. For a display I had planned, I needed a department store mannequin, and no store was willing to loan one to us. I called stores, claiming to be an employee of a different branch

65

of the chain in need of an extra mannequin. I might not have been using the right vernacular because I was rebuffed the first two or three times I spoke to a manager, but I kept them on the phone long enough to pick up some of the subtleties of the retail fashion world.

I called Stewart's on Fourth Street in Louisville and identified myself as the manager of the men's department of the store at Oxmoor Mall. Stewart's was an upscale chain in Louisville, and the manager at the Fourth Street branch was fine with me coming by that night to pick up an extra mannequin. As I grabbed my keys, and headed for my parents' car, the word "theft" popped into my head. If I got caught, it would almost certainly result in my arrest, and getting caught would be a likelihood as the stolen property would be on display for an entire school filled with kids and teachers — some of whom found my energy more than a little annoying.

So I scrapped the mannequin plan as too risky.

But I remembered a fun little interlude during football season when I drove a carload of New Albany soccer players to Providence, where we spray-painted "GO NA" and "Bulldogs Rule" among other idiotic but spirited scrawlings on signs that bordered the entrance to the school on Old Highway 62. It was a quick in-and-out operation with no fallout, minus my dad being unable to follow us after we bought the spray paint at the local Kroger and headed to the school.

This led to an uncomfortable exchange with Dad that night as he quizzed me about where I was. He caught me in a string of lies by playing dumb before finally telling me that he and my sister saw us at the Kroger and tried to tail us as I drove like an idiot toward Providence. I was passing cars on the shoulder of Charlestown Road in my mom's massive purple 1967 Buick LeSabre, which seemed to be built for this kind of adventure. It seated 10 high school students uncomfortably, had a maximum speed of 82 mph (on a good day), and its metal bumper made it more tank than car.

A second blow-by vandalism seemed like a solid way to kill a few minutes, with Dad sitting quietly at home.

I grabbed a couple of juniors in the hall and told them how much fun I had during the football assault. I didn't have to sell the idea at all. They were in when they heard "paint" and "Providence" in the same sentence. Off we went to the Kroger where we bought a can of spray paint for each of us. I stealthily parked at a nearby apartment complex adjacent to Providence because an athletic event was underway, and the parking lot was packed.

I ran to the entrance signs we painted before the football game, and repeated my extensive pro New Albany propaganda. In my enthusiasm, I lost track of my compatriots. I finished scribbling and headed for the car, but stopped cold when I saw Chris and Tommy spray painting a statue of the Virgin Mary in front of the school. The statue was very well lit, and they could be seen from the road.

I ran and shouted quietly, "Let's get the hell outta here!" Chris followed, but Tommy was locked into his work. He continued painting until we were halfway back to the car. "Hey, let's go!" Tommy bolted, and soon enough we were on our way back to the high school. I stopped at McDonald's to pick up a bunch of burgers so we would have a cover story if people wanted to know where we had been.

"Look, when we get back, we hand out the burgers," I told them. "We say nothing about what we did. It stays between the three of us no matter what happens!" Chris and Tommy agreed as they giggled. I went over it again just to be sure.

We walked back into the school, and as soon as Tommy saw a group of classmates he yelled, "You have to see what we did! We painted the Mary and everything!" Within 10 minutes, a caravan of 15 cars was headed to Providence to audit Tommy's claims of spirited vandalism. Cars of New Albany students paraded through the entrance and exit at roughly the speed of those on a tour of neighborhoods that get ambitious with Christmas lights.

This was a disaster.

The news of our work was all over school the next morning, and the student council (of which I was the co-treasurer) had offered a $100 reward for information that led to the apprehension of the miscreant vandals. The front page of the *New Albany Tribune* featured the story for days. My mom asked whether I had anything to do with it. "Me? No, I would never paint a religious icon like the Virgin Mary," I told her. That was technically true, but in spirit a bald-faced lie.

I was called to the office by the assistant principal on Thursday morning and asked if I had painted Providence along with Tommy. I thought he was fishing, so I told him that I had not. I went straight to the classroom where Tommy should have been in class. He wasn't there, so I called him at home. I repeated the conversation I had with Mr. Largent, and he told me he had confessed that morning. During his admission, he mentioned I was there too.

He just couldn't stand the strain, I guess.

Chris did the same the following day, and I heard about that from a student assistant in the office. I knew the jig was up. They had confessions from Chris and Tommy that implicated me, so I went back to the assistant principal's office and told him, "I'm not talking about anyone else, but I'll tell you what I'm responsible for. I painted 'Go NA' and

'Bulldogs Rule' on the signs out front of Providence. Nothing more."

It bears mention these shenanigans ran concurrent with my involvement in a scam to imitate a counselor's voice during phone calls to the parents of two classmates, who had dared write a letter to the editor of the student newspaper decrying the popularity of the basketball team. I said they were absent from school, and I wanted to make sure they were okay.

The calls were made in front of quite a crowd. I did a dead-on impression of the counselor and I played it straight enough that the parents bought it. As soon as I saw the 20 or so people around the phone I should have pulled the plug, but what 17-year-old passes on the opportunity to amuse?

The kids who had written the letter were serious students, so the parents went bananas trying to figure out what caused their sons to miss school that day. I thought the parents would simply quiz them about their day when they got home.

Yeah, not so much.

They called the local hospital and police, and drove the route from their houses to the school. It was another mess of my own making, and it was going to get worse because I heard the parents called the school and had a meeting scheduled with the counselor. I was also told there were students who had listened to me make the call drifting into the office. I could only assume they were tossing me to the wolves.

I've never understood the need for people to tattle on each other. As often as it happened to me in high school, you would think wisdom would seep in if only because of my proximity to so much of it. But I always trusted in in a friend or acquaintance's ability to keep a confidence.

This time, because I was the lone offender, I tried to show contrition without being prompted. I told the counselor exactly what I did and why — total transparency. I even asked what I should do to make it right. Before he answered, I said, "I really feel like I should call the two mothers I frightened." He told me that might be a good start.

I made the calls to the moms, apologizing sincerely. If my mom got a call like that, she would have assumed correctly I had decided to do something with my day other than sit at a desk staring at walls.

These guys were humorless toadies, but that didn't mean the moms deserved to have their days ruined with worry.

That meeting with the counselor was the last I ever heard about my prank phone calls. Maybe my preemptive decency won that day, or maybe I had stacked so much crap for the authorities at New Albany High School to sort through, they just decided to forget about it.

The next Monday, the principal called the families of the three Providence vandals and asked us to meet with him after school. He explained his disappointment, and accused us of living by "the code of the criminal." He was furious we had wasted the assistant principal's time, and suspended us for five days. We also had to pay $50 each to cover the cost of the sandblasting to remove the paint.

Because I had received my income tax refund of $63 the day before, I was flush. I had a $50 bill in my pocket. I flipped it onto the principal's desk to amuse my dad. The principal glared at me, and I thought I saw the hint of a smile briefly flash across Dad's face.

Half the faculty was mad that I was suspended at all and the other half wanted me expelled. There were several students who implicated me in order to get the reward. Not sure whether my co-treasurer ever wrote a check, but I certainly didn't.

Lessons learned:

1. If you are going to break rules or laws in a very public way, do it alone and keep your mouth shut.

2. Better yet, because idiocy is only fun when shared with other idiots, don't be an idiot!

3. If you know you're caught, go ahead and throw yourself on the spit as long as the consequence isn't too severe.

4. Be careful about having fun at the expense of others. Not only isn't it very nice, but those people will wait in the weeds for the opportunity to make you miserable.

Turning the Tables on Dad

As a typical teenager, I snuck out of the house every now and then to enjoy the company of friends after curfew. I was a clever kid who got away with it more often than not, but there was a night the summer after graduating high school that went very wrong. And then very right.

It started out innocently enough as eight or ten guys convened at Lewie's house to play cards and have some laughs. There was beer, too. We weren't above a little drinking to enhance the fun. The problem for me was the ever-present curfew. After high school graduation, most of the guys who had been restricted by a curfew were released. My parents still demanded I be home at a decent hour. Dad always said, "Nothing good happens after midnight." It took me my teenage years and my 20s (maybe part of my 30s, too) to embrace his lesson. I know now it's as true as anything he ever said. This night, I was supposed to be home by 11 p.m.

Just as this night was gaining momentum, I was supposed to head home. There were two problems — the guy who I rode with to Lewie's was nowhere near ready to leave, and I wasn't either. So I called my parents and explained the situation. As usual there was no wiggle room on the curfew time, and I had to decide whether defying my parents was worth a week of being grounded. This was a Saturday night, so that meant sacrificing the entire following weekend. If this had been Friday, I likely would have bitten the bullet and stayed out for as long as I liked. Instead, I decided to split the difference.

That meant getting home on time, but double-timing it back to Lewie's without my parents knowing. I asked Chris to haul me home (a seven-mile drive), wait in the car while I came in the front door, walked into my bedroom, climbed out the window, and ran back to the car. The whole operation should have taken no more than five minutes. He laughed and agreed. Chris was always eager to see me put my life in peril as I defied my parents.

I walked through the door at exactly 11 p.m. and said hi to my dad and sister, who were playing two —handed euchre. (Euchre is a mostly midwestern card game requiring four people. There is a mutation of the game that allows for three, but under no circumstance is a two-person game played. I had never seen two-handed euchre attempted before that night, and I've never heard of it since.). Dad asked if I wanted to play, and I declined. I assumed Dad and Kelly had been waiting for me to get home. They should have headed to bed right away.

Trying to be as efficient as possible, I went to my bedroom, opened the window, removed the screen, and closed the drapes before returning to the living room to try to prod Dad and Kelly into quitting their game. It was fruitless — they were enjoying themselves. It seemed cruel to keep Chris out front with his car running, so I went to the window and waved to let him know he should roll back to Lewie's without me.

Dad and Kelly wrapped their euchre marathon at 11:40 p.m., and said goodnight. When all was quiet, I stuffed pillows under my sheets in the shape of a body, jumped out the window, started my mom's car, and drove like hell back to Lewie's.

When I got there, I regaled the boys with my clever ruse and grabbed a beer.

What I didn't know was that shortly after I left, Dad popped his head in to see what I wanted for breakfast. When he got no response, Dad shook what he thought was my body. "He's gone," Dad yelled. He ran to the window, "The car's gone!"

Dad gathered my mom and sister and they headed for Lewie's in his car, where they correctly assumed I would return.

The card game continued, and we were having a great time. Lewie's house was always a great place to hang. His parents were either cool by nature or had been worn down by his two older brothers and older sister. Probably both.

Suddenly, the room got quiet. One by one, people stopped laughing. Soon, I was the only guy laughing. Lewie stared at me with a sick look on his face. "What's going on?" I asked.

Lewie said, "Clark's here." I laughed. "Stop laughing. He's in the front window staring at us right now with a giant cigar hanging out of his mouth." I turned my head slowly, as though that would make the reality of my dad standing in the window less jarring. It wasn't.

I had been down a lot of roads with Dad. During high school, I tested his patience often. But he had never confronted me like this when I was out with friends. I was flat busted as a liar by a guy who loathed lying more than anything.

I walked to the door, and greeted Dad with a wave. "Get in the car and drive home. We'll follow you," he said in a calm tone that belied his fury. I did what I was told. I rejected arguing with him on Lewie's doorstep because Dad was too competitive to invite to a public debate. My brain scrambled for a tactic that might be effective against the exasperation of a father scorned. There was a very good chance in my mind that he might kick me out of the house, and I thought about options should it come to that. As I drove, I hit upon the truth of the matter — that I was right!

Lying was wrong. Not respecting the rules of my family's house was wrong. Drinking a few beers was a little bit wrong. But being in the company of friends on a Saturday night after 11 p.m. was not wrong. I needed to man up and tell Dad that an 11 p.m. curfew was absurd for an 18-year-old high school graduate. Not only was it a reasonable position, it would likely throw Dad way off-balance. I had defied him, lied to him, baited him, and sparred with him, but I had never — *ever* — come at him with righteous indignation.

I got home first and kept the house lights off. When he, Mom, and my sister walked in, I took two steps toward him and trusted my mouth to say the right words. "This is ridiculous. You showing up at my friend's house and embarrassing me is unbelievable. What I did was defy a curfew that applies to none of my other friends. I don't know what I've done to earn this level of distrust, but it's just not right."

Dad had a look on his face I had never seen before. He was unsure of himself, and to be honest I hated that I made him look like that. Self-doubt did not become him. After a few seconds, he asked what I thought was fair.

"As long as you know where I am and with whom, I should not have a curfew. I should not be in a position where I should feel sneaking out is appropriate."

Dad replied quietly, "We'll talk about it in the morning."

My first thought was that through blaming the system — his system — I had bought myself a free night. If all hell was going to break loose, at least it wasn't going to be at 1:30 in the morning. My second thought was that my relationship with Dad would never be the same. Whether it would be better or worse, I was unsure, but it was going to change completely. I kind of enjoyed the gamesmanship of trying to extend the curfew, and occasionally defying it when it didn't suit my purposes. Looking back, one of the things I enjoyed about breaking curfew was being grounded as a result. Being unconcerned with social obligations kind of suited me, but I wasn't bold enough to enforce a personal social ban. Mom and Dad always took care of that for me.

The next morning, Dad rendered his verdict. "You'll be allowed to come and go when you want as long as we always know where you are," he said. "You're 18, but this is our house, and you'll respect our rules."

That was a big win, but I was right in believing Dad and I would enjoy a different relationship. Despite greater freedom, it wasn't nearly as contentious or fun. I was no longer going to be held to Dad's standards. In many ways, I was now on my own. That night at Lewie's was the end of my life as my father's son.

Whether I liked it or not, the pendulum had swung. I was now more adult than kid in Dad's eyes, and that was a change I didn't always care for. Being my dad's son had defined my childhood in many ways, and now it was over. It was going to happen eventually, but I wish the change had come because I behaved like an adult rather than being clever after my last act of overt defiance.

Lessons learned:

1. What annoys you as a kid might be exactly what you need.

2. Outflanking your dad isn't really a victory after all.

3. When your dad says, "Nothing good happens after midnight," he's right more often than not.

4. You are going to have a lot of friends, but only one Dad.

Losing the
Roommate Lottery

My initial roommate at Indiana University was a disaster. We had nothing in common. Gil was a stoner and speed freak, and I was not. Gil was 6'5", 235 lbs., and I was 6'0" and 147 lbs. Gil had a serious girlfriend, and I did not. I had friends on campus, and Gil did not.

Gil had one friend, Woody, from his hometown who shared Gil's craving for weed and hash. They spent an inordinate amount of time in our room getting stoned. A purposeful lack of air circulation made the room uninhabitable for me. Gil didn't go to many classes, and only stopped smoking weed when he slept.

Every other weekend, Gil's girlfriend Callie visited. This meant I was supposed to find alternate accommodations. That wasn't a problem at first, as prevailing upon friends or accepting an invitation from a girl I met at a party was okay for awhile. I never wanted to ask friends more than once, and those girls who invited me over were not options on an ongoing basis.

I know what you're thinking — a talk with Gil about boundaries would have been a solid idea. Allowing him to make my life miserable was an act of weakness bordering on cowardice. My defense is that I thought this was what college was — idiots getting stoned all the time and banging girlfriends from a nearby school. In my mind, I was responsible for my own misery because I was not the prototypical IU student.

There was always the option of going to the housing people to talk about my roommate's stash and milk jugs full of Black Beauties (speed) that he kept in the mini-fridge and sold to other students, but I am not a rat. My parents had no tolerance for tattletales, and I learned to keep my mouth shut from them. Better to just try to figure out a way to pass the time without making waves, and try to take full advantage of Gil's visits to Callie on the alternate weekend when she wasn't in Bloomington.

Gil did something nice, I thought, two months into this miserable experience. One weekend when I went home, Gil built a loft for me. I initially believed this was a generous gesture — kind of an olive branch for being a pain in the ass. A loft allows a bed to be installed six feet off the ground between desks in a dorm room to give the room occupants more space. Gil's bed remained on the floor, which struck me as strange.

"Hey, that's cool. Thanks!" I said to Gil after I came back on Sunday.

Gil was cutting hash into cubes, and barely looked up. "Yeah, good."

It took me about 45 seconds after climbing up the first time to realize what Gil had really done. He had exiled me to the upper reaches so he could have the entire room to himself. This seemed a brazen move, and for a few minutes I was really pissed off. Then I saw my banishment as a mutually beneficial reconfiguration. I could move my TV up there, hang a blanket, and pretend I was alone — except for the weed stench and inane conversation and giggling.

Laying in a loft watching a black and white TV was no way to spend time, so I became more enterprising in finding alternate activities. Former IU great Steve Downing went over game film from IU practices and games in the dorm lounge to help intramural coaches teach the game better. I sat in and soaked up as much insight as I could about man-to-man defense and motion offense — the two hallmarks of Bob Knight's basketball philosophy. I visited home periodically. I even hitchhiked one Thursday night to see a girl at Hope College in Holland, Michigan.

Robin and I were classmates at Lake Hills Elementary School in Spring Lake, Michigan, in fifth and sixth grade. We had started writing letters and talking to each other on the phone as seniors in high school, and she asked me to come up to Hope College for a dance. Without access to a car, I declined. That Thursday, I was ready to explode. Callie popped down a night early, and at 10 p.m. they decided to resist their physical urges no longer. Rather than lay in the loft while Gil and Callie engaged in their stoner version of sexual congress, I put on my Cubs jacket and bolted from the room.

On my way downstairs, I remembered the dance would be the next night. If I hitchhiked with reasonable good fortune, I could get there by the following morning. And what the hell did I have to lose. Misery in the dorm? Hope on the road to Hope. Easy choice.

What I learned hitchhiking during college was that it's a lot like craps at the casino. The dice get hot, and the dice get cold. Sometimes rides are easy — sometimes not. As a senior, I made it to Ann Arbor from Bloomington in a lightning fast five hours. This trip would not be like that.

Drivers who pick up hitchhikers, at least those who are not deranged killers, have one trait in common — they all want to talk. Every one of the 32 drivers who ferried me closer to Holland was going through a divorce, and they each told me how their marriages had unraveled. I was a stranger, didn't judge, and had no easy exit, so these drivers bared their souls to me in a way that they probably didn't with family. Even if I could have left, I wouldn't have. The stories were fascinating, and it was 10-degrees outside.

These soon-to-be former husbands were unanimous in their awareness that they caused the failures of their marriages. None were abusive — just indifferent in one way or the other to their wives. The stories were sad and endless. They would have made a good book — a depressing book, but a good one.

The first guy who picked me up on State Road 37, just west of Bloomington, introduced himself as the author of an exhaustively researched book on boxing. I asked him how long he had been working on it. "Since 1966," he said. Working on a boxing book for almost 20 years? No wonder his marriage was in tatters. He got me to Indianapolis.

One guy picked me up in Benton Harbor, Michigan. He said, "I don't pick up hitchhikers, but I'm making an exception because if you stand on the side of this road in Benton Harbor at night, you will be killed." I laughed. "Dead serious," he said. "Killed. I'm not even going this way, but I gotta get you north of town or I'll see you on the news and feel terrible." Bad town. Good guy.

Another guy started crying so hard, he had to pull off the highway into a rest stop. It occurred to me that my willingness to listen with empathy had derailed my progress. The guy composed himself, and we soldiered on. If I knew then what I know now about rest stops, I would've run into the woods.

What I learned those two nights as a hobo hitchhiker is that every person has a story, and that being alone in the dark on an interstate was more fun that being Gil's roommate. Despite the frigid weather, the uncertainty of the next ride, and my admittedly strange decision to embark on this journey, I was happy for the first time in months. I whistled, sang, and practiced impressions of celebrities — all of which sucked, but made me laugh.

Eventually, I got to Holland.

To say Robin was surprised to see me is an understatement. I called Robin from the phone in her dorm lounge:

"Hello."

"It's Kent. I'm here!"

"Where?"

"Here!"

"In Holland?"

"In your dorm's lounge."

"What?"

"I'm in your dorm."

"Why?"

"Thought I would pop up for the dance."

"Oh. I'll be right up."

It had dawned on me this surprise visit was a bad idea somewhere near the Indiana-Michigan state line, but I was already pot committed. I had no toiletries or change of clothes. Being accompanied to a dance by an unwashed guy carrying the aroma of 32 different cars and trucks who Robin had not seen since the sixth grade was likely not something she would be enthusiastic about.

She wasn't.

Robin was very polite about telling me her parents were taking her to dinner. There was no chance I would be invited to the dinner. We talked for an hour, and then I hit the road back to Bloomington, sparing both of us the awkwardness of my continued presence.

This trip was more productive and enjoyable than what I would have endured in my dorm room with Gil and Callie — a lot more fun. In the abstract, watching other people have sex seems like it might be a good time. People pay for the privilege to watch porn, and this was a live show! But it was a terrible live show featuring two players I disliked.

Coming back from Christmas Break, I decided that there would not be a repeat of my first semester misery. The first Saturday night back, a friend named Lee and I got a pizza. He said, "Gil's got Callie this weekend, right? Better go to my room." I told him there wouldn't be a problem in my room. Lee was a little leery, but up we went.

I put my key in the lock, turned the knob, and opened the door.

"Get outta here!" Gil yelled as he leaped from the bed in his jockey shorts and tried to slam the door.

I pushed my way in, "I got a pizza. We're eating it here."

Gil was a big guy, and he grabbed me be the neck and pinned me against the door across the hall, "Callie's here. You even try to eat that pizza in there, and I'll beat your ass."

I yelled back, "You better kill me because if you don't, there'll come a night when I decide it's my turn. I'll take a baseball bat to your knees." He kept screaming, I kept screaming, and to be honest I don't remember where the hell we ate the pizza.

Two weekends later I went home to celebrate my birthday, and when Dad brought me back to the dorm he mentioned he would like to come up to the room. I thought this had a pretty good chance of being interesting. Sunday afternoon when Callie visited was a lock for them to be doing something that would infuriate my dad.

I put my key in the lock, and Gil yelled, "Come back later!"

I turned the key, and opened the door. The room, as usual, was hazy with weed smoke, Gil was in his jockeys, and Callie was topless. When Gil saw my dad, he went from furious to baffled. Dad looked around the room for what seemed like quite awhile, closed the door, and said, "Tomorrow, talk to the housing people and get the hell out of that room."

The next day, I walked into the housing coordinator's office and told him I needed to move. When he asked why, I said, "Roommate behavior." He knew my vagueness was purposeful, and didn't press for details that might cause him more work than filling out a room change form. The coordinator showed me a list of available rooms, and there was a double —single on the ninth floor that caught my eye. Lee lived on that floor, and I knew a few guys up there a little bit. Seemed like a good fit.

I moved to the ninth floor, and all of a sudden college made sense. The people on my new floor were reasonable human beings — smart, funny, and not content to live life stoned. I stayed with and around Larry, Hoss, Mote, Spanky, Sid, and Suey for the rest of my college years. Larry became the godfather to my son, and I still see all of them occasionally.

In the moment, I questioned my willingness to acquiesce to Gil — a moron of the first order. To be honest I'm still not thrilled that I allowed him to dictate terms in the way he did. I should have stopped it one way or the other. But by being patient — or weak, if you prefer — the timing became right for me to be relocated to the perfect spot where I met lifelong friends.

Timing is the key to solving all problems. Being patient allows the correct solution to reveal itself. Trying to solve problems as quickly as they pop up sometimes causes more serious problems.

There are times in life when nothing is easy. Even when things should be easy, I embrace allowing them to become difficult. Not sure whether it's because I'm a boob or love a challenge more than an easy win, but I love a tough challenge. Far more often than not, embracing a challenge is more rewarding than taking the clear and unimpeded path to an obvious victory. Even if you feel like a moron in the moment, the hard road is usually the best road.

Lessons learned:

1. Life is not a contest to see how much garbage you can eat. If you are miserable — exit.

2. Live only with people who share your appetites for intoxicants. Living with a stoner — if you are not a stoner — is not going to work. And vice-versa.

3. Don't hitchhike! It's dangerous out there.

Attention Kmart Shoppers!

There were two responsibilities I enjoyed during my four months working for Kmart while a college student. The first was peering at potential shoplifters through a two-way mirror above the automotive department, and the other was hosting Blue Light Specials.

Kmarts have virtually disappeared from the American retail landscape, but back in the 1980s, they were everywhere, and one of their big allures was the occasional instant special that was accompanied by a flashing blue light. They lasted for 15 minutes, and employees were empowered to activate Blue Light Specials within their departments upon their whim from a list approved by management.

I never caught a thief, but I sure as hell went nuts with Blue Light Specials! "Attention Kmart shoppers, I'd like to direct your attention to the automotive department where for the next 15 minutes we will feature Prestone antifreeze at the low, low Kmart price of $1.29 for a half gallon bottle. Again, that's Prestone antifreeze at $1.29 for the next 15 minutes in our automotive department, and as always thank you for shopping Kmart." That was the text, and I read it at least three times each shift.

My Blue Light Specials came so fast and furious that the store manager, whom I never actually met, called to ask that I do fewer of them. My motivation for getting on the paging system had nothing to do with providing shoppers with great deals on antifreeze — I just wanted to yammer on the paging system. It was hilarious to me that I could interrupt the crappy music that normally blared throughout the store anytime I liked with my own little show.

The code to activate the paging system via the phones throughout the store was *5. That was easy enough to remember, and the code was the same for every Kmart.

You can probably see where this is headed. Yep, dropping in to announce Blue Light Specials with absurdly low prices were a must-do anytime I drove by a Kmart. "Attention Kmart shoppers, I'd like to direct your attention to our watch and jewelry department, where for the next 15 minutes we will celebrate our love for our customers with a very special price of $29.95 on all of our Rolex timepieces. Again, that's the Rolex of your choice for $29.95 as a token of our appreciation for the next 15 minutes in our watch and jewelry department, and as always, thank you for shopping Kmart."

Obviously, Kmart has never sold Rolexes, so there was no legal issue with people demanding the preposterous price on a luxury timepiece. Eventually my amusement in activating fake Blue Light Specials ended, but that didn't mean an end to fun with the paging system. Every once in a while I would see someone I knew at the Kmart near Indiana University in Bloomington, and paging that person by name to walk to a department across the store was a great source of hilarity.

One summer afternoon, as Julie and I shopped for discount goods, I saw a guy named C.J. Miller who had lived on my dorm floor a few years earlier. He was in the checkout lane with a cart full of plants. I ran to one of the phones, pressed *5, and said, "Attention Kmart shoppers, would C.J. Miller please report to the home and garden department. C. J. Miller to home and garden." C.J. looked confused, but dutifully pushed his cart to the home and garden section in the far corner of the store. It was probably an 80-yard walk.

We followed and watched C.J. search in vain for an employee who might have demanded his presence. He waited for a three or four minutes, then hiked back to the cashier. As he got to the front of the line — again, I paged him back to home and garden. C.J. threw his arms in the air and stormed to the far corner of the store a second time. There was no waiting patiently for a clerk this time. He sought out Kmart employees and aggressively asked three different people why he had been paged. Borderline furious after not getting an explanation, C.J. muttered to himself on that long walk back to the only lane open at the front of the store.

Because I wanted to come clean to C.J. and say hello, I told Julie I would page him one more time, and then out myself as the perpetrator of this practical joke. Julie shared her opinion that this was not a great idea — that C.J. was very upset, and hearing another page might just send him into a violent rage. I told Julie all funny things come in sets of three. It wasn't my rule, and who was I to argue with the gods of humor.

Predictably, C.J. was most displeased to hear his name over the paging system a third time. This time, he practically ran from the cashier station. I walked toward him, "C.J.! C.J.!" I was laughing and tried to explain, but he didn't hear a word. He ran past me without making eye contact. As he passed, I yelled his name after him, "C.J.!" He never broke stride.

Julie and I looked at each other, and I said, "Let's get the hell out of here." Nothing good was going to come from a confession to a guy whose anger was so profound that he had lost the ability to hear his name when spoken directly to him.

I never saw C.J. again, and hope he doesn't swear out his revenge if he ever reads this. It was all in fun, C.J.!

Not satisfied with tormenting C.J., five years later I did the same thing in Chicago to another old friend who we happened to see in the checkout lane at the Jewel Grocery Store at the corner of Ashland and Wellington. Mavis Frangel waited behind four shoppers as we waited in line three lanes to the left. As Mavis began off-loading her cart, I found a phone and paged her to customer service. She removed her items from the conveyor and pushed the cart to customer service, where she waited in line behind customers who were either returning items, buying lottery tickets, or asking inane questions (I deduce this from my experience waiting for customer service assistance). She finally reached the front of that line as we finished checking out. The customer service specialist convinced Mavis that she had not been paged by anyone in her area, so Mavis moved her cart back to the cashier's lane she had abandoned when paged. There were another four people in front of her.

I gave serious thought to going back for a second turn of paging Mavis, but decided not to be a total tool about it. I guess that could be called progress by some. Others would say my empathy for Mavis was regression.

My days of paging friends ended at the Jewel, but that didn't mean I was through causing retail mayhem through bizarre announcements. As Julie and I visited her family in Griffith, Indiana, I would duck out of the house for an hour to roam around town. I always found myself at the Venture store, which was nothing more than a Kmart by another name, and no, it did not smell as sweet.

The paging system at Venture wasn't tough to crack — it was taped to the phone. I would walk around the store, committing to memory the names of clerks, cashiers, and stock people. Then, in an unholy barrage of pages separated by 20-30 seconds, I would shift the entire staff to different departments. Cashiers were told to abandon their lanes to see the manager, customer service people were sent to a specific aisle, and stock people criss-crossed the store from one department to another.

To conceal my identity, I made each page from a different phone. That was almost certainly an unnecessary security measure, as the people working for minimum wage at Venture didn't appear to be qualified to locate and hold accountable the Jason Bourne of department store pranksters. I would return to the in-laws house amused by my shenanigans and ready for an afternoon of watching PBS — the network of choice at the Purcell home.

I talk about my dad's influence on me throughout this book, but this is one area where I taught my dad a little something about self-amusement to escape boredom. As my mom shopped at a JC Penney's, I asked Dad if he wanted to have some fun. I was 14 at the time, and Dad probably questioned whether I knew much about having fun. He said sure, why not.

Obviously, this was long before smart phones gave each of us our own alarm clock. People would buy alarm clocks and clock radios, and different models were displayed by the dozen in the electronics department. All those clocks, all those alarms.

It was 8:15 p.m. when I told Dad we were going to quietly set all the alarms to 8:23 p.m. without drawing attention to ourselves. The area was fairly congested, so moving from clock to clock without people noticing was easy enough. It took five or six minutes to get them all set correctly. After we finished, Dad asked "Why 8:23? Why not 8:30?"

"Who wants to wait an extra seven minutes?" I answered.

We waited, and one alarm buzzed, then a second beeped, and a third rang. Within a minute, the cacophony was loud, obnoxious, and hilarious. The electronics department staff of one ran through the clock area shutting off alarms for the next 10 minutes, and we laughed from the next level. When we found Mom, she had finished her shopping, and we had successfully killed the time needed for her to find a top, pair of shoes, or whatever else she might have been looking for — a win-win!

Sadly, technology has rendered alarm clocks, clock radios, and paging systems dinosaurs in the retail game. Many stores communicate directly with employees via earpieces. Others simply text. There are still a few stores where people can be paged, but it's hardly worth the long drive just for a few laughs.

The 1980s and 1990s were simpler times, when time could be killed through benign but clever malevolence. Now, we sit idly and read on our smart phones whatever Twitter, Facebook, and ESPN have to offer.

They call that progress?

Lessons learned:

1. Be careful going to the well for the same practical jokes too often.

2. Having fun with your brain — even at the expense of others — is a lot more fun than staring at a smartphone.

3. Father and son fun doesn't require golf, tickets to a ball game, or an expensive steak.

4. If you're bored, you just aren't trying.

Take the Long Way Home

My misery at Indiana University during the fall of 1983 was immeasurable. After a blissful summer as a camp counselor, I returned to school a new man in an old environment. My roommates were coke-fueled tools, friends were across town, and I didn't have a girlfriend.

My junior year was difficult — the kind many college students have — the one you survive so you can enjoy the others. I had plenty of good times in college, but none of them came during the 1983-1984 school year. Things got so bad at the end of January that I developed gallstones, which had to be removed, causing my withdrawal from IU.

Among the incidents that either caused or reflected my misery:

I hitchhiked to the University of Michigan one Friday night, and came back the following Tuesday after a detour to the University of Illinois.

I awakened early on a Saturday morning to the site of female breasts next to my face — normally a positive, but not when the owner is on a whiskey and cocaine bender.

I was duped into being a stooge in a racket to steal frozen pizzas at a 7-11. I had no idea what my roommate was doing. He told me to talk to the cashier until he left. I should have guessed he was doing something idiotic and criminal.

My roommate calmly explained one night that by living in our apartment I had become an accessory after the fact to coke possession or sale, or whatever the hell was happening with the coke.

To add insult to injury, the White Sox won the American League West.

My one happy place was on my bike. Two summers prior to that school year, I worked for six weeks pressing veneer (not a euphemism) to earn enough cash to buy a decent bicycle. It was a black Schwinn Voyageur 11.8 that cost $350. I rode it everywhere. Flying around Bloomington on something I worked to buy gave me a strange sense of satisfaction and freedom. Alone with my thoughts on a racing bike, I still feel totally at peace.

One Friday morning after a Thursday night of beers, I decided a weekend at home with family was a good idea. I didn't have a car and no one from New Albany that I knew was headed home, so I decided to hop on my bike and ride. The distance between the apartment in Bloomington and our home in New Albany was 92 miles, and I had wanted to try riding a solid 100 miles since I read a magazine article about how hard it is to crack the century mark. The training recommended seemed way overblown, so to do it as an ordinary guy who was slightly hungover and had never trained to ride 100 miles in one stretch seemed a great challenge.

The most direct route was State Road 37 to State Road 60, and bicycles were allowed on both highways. So off I went — without breakfast and more than a little parched. The pedaling was oddly difficult from the first stroke, which I ascribed to the beers from the night before. I got to 37 and headed south toward Bedford while continuing to labor. I thought about turning around, but refused — not out of grit, but because another weekend in Bloomington was an unbearable thought. Naked coked-up co-eds in a bedroom might appeal to some, but to me it was evidence of my roommates' toxicity. I didn't want to pity nude women standing next to my bed ever again, so I kept churning.

As I passed the 10-mile mark, I noticed that I was slowing down as I coasted downhill. Either my bike had ceased obeying the immutable laws of physics, or my brakes were rubbing on the wheel. I stopped the bike, checked, and sure enough the rear brakes needed to be adjusted. Once that was squared away, the riding was easy.

As I flew through Bedford, the endorphins kicked in and my legs churned like perpetual motion machines. I thought maybe I would ride right through New Albany and continue south forever.

Sadly, those dreams were dashed just south of Mitchell, Indiana, (the home of astronaut Gus Grissom, according to signage surrounding the town) as my thirst and hunger became an issue. Not only did I leave Bloomington with a hangover, I also left with only three dollars. A real meal was out of the question, and water needed to be suckled from men's room faucets (a thought that makes me vomit in my mouth as I type it).

The lack of water and food first caused cramping in my calves, but I continued on. I stopped at a McDonald's, got a Big Mac and small Coke, and tried to will myself to soldier forward toward New Albany fortified by the emptiest calories a human being can consume. I made it another 10 miles before the cramps returned to my calves and spread to my quadriceps. Pedaling with frozen calves is possible, but quads are essential to making the pedals turn.

I fell off my bike onto a lawn in Salem and rubbed my legs. Maybe with a team of massage therapists I would have been able to quickly rebound for the remaining 30 miles, but with only two hands — each with pinkies numbed from gripping the handlebars, I could only do so much. Every cycle of the pedals was a struggle worse than when my brakes rubbed against the rear wheel.

Another 15 miles down the road at the Kimball plant in Borden I suffered complete muscle failure. The only positive was that the failure did not extend to my bowels, as we occasionally see on TV coverage of triathlons. At the plant, I walked stiff-legged like a fit and smaller version of Frankenstein's monster, and asked the receptionist if I could make a phone call. She appeared a bit stunned by my haggard appearance and bizarre gait, and allowed my phone call.

I told Dad that I was 15 miles up the road, and sure could use a ride. He asked how I had gotten there. "On my bike," I answered. Dad laughed as dads do when sons do something especially idiotic. Fifteen minutes later, both Mom and Dad were there to scrape the remains of their son off the parking lot pavement and into the backseat.

After spending a nice, quiet weekend at home eating food far better than my usual fare of hotdogs or Totino's frozen pizza, Dad hauled me back to my miserable existence in Bloomington.

I've always wondered whether I would have made the 92 mile ride home if my brakes had been correctly adjusted from the beginning of the ride, and I finally understood why athletes enjoy the kind of distance races that appear to the rest of us as painful wastes of effort and time. It's not just about the test of the event; it's the endorphins that make you feel strong as hell. I mean super —hero strong. It's also wonderful to be utterly alone with your thoughts, moving only through the efforts of a body that has been prepared — at least partially — for hours of exertion.

Unhappiness prompts a lot of strange behavior and activities, and that bike ride was likely the most productive of my college era. It also might have been significantly dangerous and irresponsible given that I didn't wear a helmet and never told anyone I was going on this expedition. There is also the potential for mayhem — either being hit by a car or shot by some nut looking for some live target practice.

People are fond of saying those suffering through unhappy times need to keep breathing, moving, and thinking. That's absolutely true, as I found out in 1983 and 1984. Author John Irving referred to it as the process of "passing the open windows" in *The Hotel New Hampshire*.

That day in the Fall of 1983, I passed open windows through southern Indiana at about 18 miles an hour until my legs finally surrendered to fatigue.

Lessons learned:

1. Drinking beer as a carb load the night before a big ride or run is either best done in moderation or is a myth entirely.

2. Extreme physical exertion as a response to fleeting anguish is not the best response, but it isn't the worst either.

3. Don't live with cokeheads or coke dealers.

4. Keep passing the open windows.

Midnight Mass with the Sterling Family

Church was a big deal for part of my family, and not a priority for the other. Dad only attended church for weddings and funerals, Mom's side of the family was Irish Catholic to the core, and my sister and I were raised Catholic but never really embraced it as our life's guiding light. Dad's family was not only not Catholic, they were not very fond of Catholics. My Uncle Bob referred to Mom as a "fish-eater" before she married Dad.

Dad rarely sat quietly for an hour unless he fell asleep in his favorite chair. His attention span would not accommodate an entire mass — or even a significant portion of one. Alone with his thoughts was not an interesting place to be for Dad. He liked entertainment. Funny worked for him. Spiritual repose did not.

My grandmother (mom's mom) visited for Christmas in 1983, and the possibility of the entire family going to mass was discussed. Looking back, I can't believe everyone agreed to go. Unanimity was almost never accomplished in my family. Our fuel was competition, and in the absence of games or sports, arguments sufficed, so there was always at least one loud dissenter.

Dad and May-May were bound by their shared love for Mom, and also their relentless disagreements on all other matters.

It was during this visit that Dad dropped the nuclear option during one of their unending political arguments. Dad was a staunch republican, and the world has never produced a more perfect and passionate democrat than my grandmother. Those two were built to argue with one another. They relished the opportunity to state their cases and belittle the other. Each argument was close to identical to the previous one — almost verbatim. My grandmother and father were to family political arguments as the Barrymores were to Broadway theater. The arguments were performed with energy and followed the same structure every time — until this one, which was to be their greatest and most insane triumph, because Dad had a special prop that would bring the curtain down on this long-running show.

Dad would begin by maligning the social programs of President Franklin Roosevelt. My grandmother would claim Roosevelt's social plans ended the great depression of the 1930s. Dad would cruelly mock Eleanor Roosevelt. My grandmother would harangue Richard Nixon's presidency as soulless and bereft of morality. Then Dad would start in on the adulterous exploits of President John F. Kennedy, which to an Irish Catholic like my grandmother was treasonous. Every single time in my life I saw my grandmother angry occurred at the end of these clashes.

So, as always, Dad went after Kennedy and his legendary infidelities, and when my grandmother leaped to his defense by invoking Kennedy's widow Jackie, Dad quickly bolted from the table yelling, "You want to see your precious Jacqueline Kennedy? I'll show you Jackie Kennedy!"

Of the dozens if not hundreds of arguments in which my dad and my grandmother engaged, this had never happened. Dad was leaving the stage for a moment. My sister and I looked at each other with anticipation. Would this be hilarious, horrifying, or both? Dad was not generally a prop debater. Words used mercilessly were his scalpel, but over the years he might have become bored with the holiday stagings of this family drama that would have made Eugene O'Neill proud. What he used to slice and dice my grandmother's adulation for Kennedy marked a first for my family.

Dad ran back to the dining room holding open a copy of Hustler (the raunchiest of all publicly sold porn mags) to a page showing a somewhat grainy nude photo of Jackie on an island beach near Greece. My grandmother's head turned purple as she laid into Dad about bringing smut into the home of her daughter and grandchildren. Dad laughed and laughed.

My memory gets foggy after that. I found these quarrels oddly entertaining. It was like watching *Caddyshack* for the 200th time. I knew the script by heart, but the commitment to the material was so complete, it was impossible not to be entertained. I felt a measure of guilt in laughing at the insanity of these two people I loved who tried to make each other feel foolish.

On Christmas Eve during this visit after tempers had cooled and the Hustler was thrown in the trash (I assume), we piled into Dad's two-tone Chevy Caprice for the drive to St. Mary's of the Knobs Catholic Church for what is called Midnight Mass, but actually begins earlier in the evening. As was the case with almost every family excursion, we were a little late. Mom would forget her purse, get caught on the phone, or somehow make us slightly late. Most of the time, that was fine. Punctuality based on a need to get somewhere at some arbitrary time is silly, but this was Midnight Mass, when even lapsed Catholics find their way into a pew for some standing, sitting, kneeling, and praying.

We got to the church just as the mass began, but all the seats were taken and many people stood near the door. Dad was agitated because being late cost us an opportunity to sit, even worse it was below zero outside with a howling wind, and every time the door was opened a blast of cold air chilled us to the bone. My grandmother was 82 at this point, and Dad had survived multiple heart attacks and quadruple bypass surgery. Extreme cold wasn't just unpleasant, it was a health hazard.

Mass began, people continued to open the door every half minute or so, and finally Dad had enough. When the door opened once too often for Dad he yelled, "Jesus Christ, shut the Goddamned door!"

I don't remember exactly what portion of the mass Dad interrupted, but the priest stopped, the entire congregation turned their heads, and all eyes were on us. There was total silence for what seemed like 15 minutes, but was probably more like three seconds. Without making eye contact with anyone, including each other, we spun and walked briskly through those same doors into the bitter cold night. As chilly as it was outside, it was far colder inside for us.

It was our good fortune that we rarely went to church, so the chance of anyone recognizing us was remote. I felt guilty because I was thrilled that we self-expelled. From what I could tell, Dad was both amused at his eruption and still a little angry at the impudence of the parishioners who had the temerity to cause us a chilly second or two. My grandmother was briefly furious and then we started laughing for two reasons — it was an all-time bizarre moment for a family that authored its fair share of those, and it was really funny in an "All in the Family" sort of way.

If *Seinfeld* character George Costanza had been Catholic, his father Frank would have done the exact same thing. If you had a low tolerance for the awkward, Dad wasn't always easy to be around, but there was always a likelihood that he would do something memorable to make you laugh. Whether it was at someone's expense was not of any interest to him. He was entertaining as hell, but I'm fairly certain my grandmother failed to see him in that light.

Memories of a moment that absurd evidently fade over time, as 12 years later my sister was married in that same church.

Lessons learned:

1. If two people you love continue to drag each other into revealing their worst selves, try to change the subject instead of embracing it as entertainment.

2. Get to church 10 minutes early so you can get a seat.

3. Never bring a hardened non-Catholic to Midnight Mass

4. No porn in the house — especially as a debate prop!

Dropping an F-bomb on Eighth Graders

Despite their ability to stun a classroom of students into obedience, f-bombs are not approved for use in the classroom by a teacher. That axiom should be self-evident to all teachers. I had to learn that lesson the hard way.

I can't remember who told me being a substitute teacher was easy cash, but as I recovered from getting my gallbladder removed it seemed like a good idea. Given my behavioral lapses as a high school student just four years before, I thought my candidacy for a position was a longshot.

Applying would never have occurred to me except I was told not to lift anything over 10 pounds for a few weeks after surgery. This was back in the day when gallbladder removal required a lengthy incision rather than arthroscopy. It was major surgery, and required that I withdraw from Indiana University for the remainder of the spring semester. With six weeks to Spring Break in 1984, it appeared I might be able to have my cake and eat it too by not going to school but still bounce to Florida with friends.

Needing money, I shaved and showed up at the New Albany-Floyd County Schools Administration Building. The assistant superintendent's enthusiasm to help complete the application meant two things were true — they were short of available subs, and all that talk about my permanent record was total BS. I filled out an application, handed over my college transcript, and was told they would be in contact whenever they needed me. I would be paid $30 per day for babysitting junior high and high school kids.

Becoming a substitute teacher gave karma two opportunities — for me to be tormented in the same way I had treated subs, and/or for me to rep all subs by bringing exactly the level of discipline I should have been subjected to just a few years before.

The phone rang the next day with a request that I report that morning to Scribner Junior High to take Mr. O'Rear's shop class. When my family first moved to New Albany, I was an eighth grader. One of my first classes was shop with Mr. O'Rear. I happily said I would be there on time and would require no directions. I knew my way to that room.

Mr. O'Rear had a great sense of humor, and he was famous for straying a bit from the typical shop curriculum in quizzes and tests. My favorite diversion was included in a quiz I administered to all six classes that day. The last question was oral — "Please spell Philadelphia." New Albany is a city just across the Ohio River from Louisville, and many of its citizens can spell Philadelphia. Apparently none of them took shop from Mr. O'Rear. In first period, not only did none of the 22 students spell Philadelphia correctly, none of the 22 versions were the same.

Six periods, 130+ students, and none spelled Philadelphia correctly. I remember when I was in the class, Mr. O'Rear was oddly impressed I spelled it correctly, "Sterling, maybe you have a chance to be a functional human being!" I was baffled. Having spent a good portion of my youth reading the sports section and sorting baseball cards, Philadelphia was impossible to avoid, so of course I could spell it correctly.

In the last period, the kids were getting loud and unruly. I brokered peace by promising they could play music for the final 10 minutes of class if they stayed quiet until then. My condition was that once the music started, if they saw Principal Beyl walking toward class, they would shut off the music and hustle back to their seats. The classroom had an outdoor entrance and anyone approaching the room could be seen a good four seconds before they got to the door. Sure enough, Mr. Beyl showed up with about six minutes left in the school day. A kid yelled, "Beyl!", and the class went from party time to orderly before he opened the door. Mr. Beyl looked confused, then smiled, "Okay. Just wanted to make sure everything is going well back here, Mr. Sterling." I assured him we were fine.

One day in, I was the cool sub who understood the minds of 14-year-olds. I felt like maybe I should be a teacher. The next day, I filled in again for Mr. O'Rear. The kids in the last class of the day talked me into allowing them to walk through the workshop. Despite warnings not to allow this, I didn't see the harm. The kids had been good, so what the hell. We were bro's, right? They wouldn't make me regret it, would they?

Of course, they did. The next morning, I got a call from the school asking if I had allowed kids into the workshop, and I told them I had — just for a few minutes. Seems a bunch of tools were missing and presumed stolen. I had been played. Lesson learned.

Day 3 as a sub came the following week at New Albany High School. I would teach English, and there were no directions from the regular teacher. I learned being friends was bad for business from the thieves in my eighth grade shop class, so I demanded quiet studying. The only challenging moment came during lunch. I didn't know where to sit in the cafeteria — with the students or the teachers — some of whom remembered me less than kindly. Tom Weatherston was my sophomore English teacher, and offered a spot at the faculty table, "Kent, come sit over here with us." I happily bounced over, grabbed a seat, and nodded my thanks. Weatherston then turned to Richard Wardell, who was my senior English teacher and said, "You remember Kent Sterling, don't you Dick?"

Wardell never looked up from his tomato soup. "Yes." His English class was an exercise in misery for me. We studied *Beowulf, Paradise Lost, The Canterbury Tales* and other indecipherable arcane texts. There was no humor to the instruction, and I spent virtually every class writing notes back and forth with Michelle, who sat in the desk behind me. I probably learned more about writing by scribbling notes to Michelle that year than by reading Chaucer, Milton, and whoever penned *Beowulf.*

So Wardell didn't care for me any more as a substitute teacher than he did when I was in his class. That was cool by me.

My fourth day was a trip back to Scribner to fill in for social studies teacher Miss Coverdale, who was my homeroom and world history teacher in the ninth grade. This was the day I began to hone my skills of commanding a classroom. In fifth period, I busted a troublemaker with a little ill temper. That class behaved immaculately from that point forward, and so did the next class. It reminded me of how kids talk between classes, especially about the temperament of subs. I decided because of my success I would begin each day with a first period tantrum to set the tone for the rest of the day.

My fifth and final day as a substitute was incredibly easy. I executed my plan to perfection as an eighth grade teacher at Hazelwood Junior High. Wearing bright orange pants and a royal blue shirt, I looked like a clown. It was for a reason. Dressing like some kind of colorblind nut would make my moment of furious discipline against the first kid who defied my demands even more effective.

The first period troublemaker made himself obvious within the first five minutes of the day. Moments after telling my first group of students they were to remain seated and quiet, I began taking attendance. As I called the name of the daughter of the principal at New Albany High School, a screwball named Morgan jumped up and shouted at another kid in the back row. This was it — my time to shut down Morgan and establish myself as a sub not to be trifled with.

I yelled, "Goddamn it! Shut up and sit the fuck down!" Oops.

The room entered an eerie realm of silence, and Morgan looked like he had been tased. He was frozen. I calmly restated my directive to sit down — this time without the F-bomb. Morgan slowly sat.

I had to stop for a moment to replay in my head what I said, hoping that I had actually not used that word. The F-bomb. Holy crap, I had never even heard a kid drop an F-bomb in a classroom, much less a teacher. Even subs are more disciplined than that. The replay was damning. I plowed through that class as though everything was just fine.

Roughly 150 eighth graders quietly passed through my door for the next six hours. They avoided eye contact with me, and read silently. The children weren't just orderly — they were scared, and scared kids get chatty. They were likely to discuss the reason for their fear with everyone they know. No way other teachers wouldn't hear the story of the psychotic sub. I was a dead teacher walking. The only question now was whether I would make it through the end of the day.

As a student, I had spent many nervous moments waiting for the assistant principal to grab me during a class, but I thought those days had ended when I graduated. Every time someone came to the door that day, I was certain he or she was there to usher me to the parking lot. Given the magnitude of my verbal slip, I wasn't sure what punishment awaited me. Was it illegal for a teacher to drop an F-bomb during class. Maybe the state legislature hadn't considered it a possibility until I did it, and a new law might be named for me. What a source of pride that would be for the Sterlings!

I know what I would have done had I been a student in that first period class — tell all my friends about the sub who went haywire, and then repeat the story to my parents at dinner. They would have camped at the principal's office the next morning to demand the teacher's termination.

Speaking of which, I remembered the high school principal's daughter was sitting to my left in the fourth row during first period as I laid down the law. She would certainly mention my irate slip of the tongue to her dad. He and I hadn't been on great terms when I was a student. Making sure I never taught again wasn't just going to be fun for him, it was the right thing to do.

I assume there were at least a few phone calls between administrators that week, although my only communication with the New Albany-Floyd County School Corporation was the same silence I craved in the classroom. I never heard from them, which was fine by me. I knew I screwed the pooch, and didn't need to be chastised by some bureaucrat for dropping an F-bomb in class.

New Albany-Floyd County Schools paid me the $150 for five days work, which seemed righteous given that prosecution and public humiliation was likely considered. That cash was enough to go to Florida in a few weeks, and that's what I really wanted.

And I assume that my permanent record was amended to reflect my profane outburst.

Lessons learned:

1. Don't hire a recent high school grad with a sketchy behavioral record to teach high school! (This is for school administrators)

2. Don't drop F-bombs in class — in fact, don't say anything in class as a teacher you never heard as a student.

3. Obedience is not the goal for a teacher — the goal should be engagement.

4. If you were bored in school as a student, what the hell do you believe you'll be as a teacher?

Killing Time at Indiana University

Here's some bad news for parents of college students — if your child carries a schedule necessary to graduate in four years and never misses a class, he or she will have 153 free hours per week. Subtract eight hours per night for sleep, and there are still 97 hours to fill. Throw in three meals at one hour per, and they still have more than 10 hours per day to study. If your kid is incredibly diligent and studies two hours for every hour in the classroom — as recommended by educators — there are still four hours a day without any purpose that need to be dealt with.

Nothing scares the hell out of college parents more than a surplus of free time because that's where the fun resides. The danger lurks there too. My dad used to say, "We aren't writing checks so you can screw around all day. You do that at home, and it doesn't cost us a cent."

Dad, as usual, was right. But here is the truly horrifying aspect of a kid having nothing to do but screw around for four hours per day. Multiply the boundless energy of college students by that four hours of free time to the power of the number of students in the university, and that equals uh-oh. I was full of uh-oh in college, and the more uh-oh the better.

My primary stock in trade was the practical joke, and I enjoyed the slow payoff. Pulling a chair out as a guy sat down lacked creativity and grace. Those types of jokes insult creativity and intellect. There was one exception to my aversion to the immediate reward in fun I had with friends. That was driving through puddles to splash students walking to class. This was an obnoxious ritual throughout college that we extended to alumni events in the name of nostalgia. Skill and brains were unnecessary. This was Looney Tunes level hilarity with the only consequence being drenched frat guys and sorority girls.

There were four great puddles on Indiana University's Bloomington campus, and they were spread out so that we could drive through all four repeatedly and never hit the same group of students twice.

The best time for splashing was immediately after a quick-moving storm dumped a half inch or more of rain and was replaced by sunny skies. A long-lasting rain discouraged walkers, but sunshine after a storm left the sidewalks filled with soon-to-be drenched freshmen. The most satisfying moment was when the walkers recognized our car was purposefully accelerating toward a giant puddle and there was no escape for them. The look of abject resignation on their faces was our moment of zen.

Of course, splashing people was weather dependent, so other time-killing and harmless diversions were developed. During Christmas Break our sophomore year, our Iranian neighbor Arman could not return to his home country. Arman was smart as hell, easily bored, and had more than three weeks each winter without classes or any responsibility. He spent that free time fabricating a device that could open the exterior doors of a dormitory elevator with nothing but a heavy gauge wire coat hanger.

You're likely wondering what enjoyment could come from the ability to open an elevator from the outside. I wondered, too, and asked Arman. "There is a manual override on the top of the elevator that we can use for a variety of purposes — sneaking a keg in the dorm without fear of stopping at another floor before we can offload it on the ninth floor — or simply scaring the hell out of people."

I was intrigued by the idea of scaring people. Arman smiled, and asked me to join him. Rick also wanted in, so we gathered at the elevator. Arman told me to get on the elevator and get it to stop on the eighth floor. While it was stopped on eight, Arman would insert his coat hanger, pop open the door, step onto the top of the elevator, and flip the switch to manual. I took the stairs from eight to nine, and joined them on the top of the elevator.

"See, what I do is allow the elevator to operate on automatic until it stops on one of the girls floors, and three or more girls get in," Arman explained. "For some reason, groups of three or four work best. When we get roughly halfway down, I flip the switch to manual, and immediately press the 'up' button. The change of direction without explanation scares them quite severely, and they scream.

"Then, I return it to automatic, and they believe either the elevator suffered a technological malfunction, or that it is possessed by the devil. You'll be surprised how many believe an elevator's direction can be altered by demons."

I should be embarrassed by the number of hours we killed by riding atop the elevators of our dorm, but I'm not. These episodes of causing girls to scream — or not — were all unique. Some screamed loudly, others grabbed the rails on the elevator walls, and some just kicked back and rode it out trusting there was no danger. It was all good fun, and no one was ever in any danger, except for us if we had fallen from an elevator top. That seemed unlikely, as I rarely fall down when I stand.

One of my favorite days of the school calendar came when the student phone directories were distributed. Those books were gold for someone who wanted to cause a little chaos with prank phone calls. My two favorite prank call schemes were time-consuming but fun.

Fraternities recruiting freshmen would invite them to introductory dinners where they might be enticed to pledge as potential members. I did my part by inviting every male freshman on Indiana's campus whose name began with the letter A (somewhere between 200-250 guys) to the Beta Theta Pi house for dinner, beer, and Monday Night Football. I told each freshman they would be treated to a 16-ounce cut of prime rib, buttery mashed potatoes, garlic toast, asparagus tips, and apple pie along with all the beer they could drink. I told them to be at the house in a sport coat and slacks by 5 p.m. sharp for a social hour with all the members. Dinner would follow at six.

This took hours, and each call was punctuated with great praise based upon their hometown, which for some reason was included in the student directory, "You know, we only invite the best and the brightest, and the swath you cut at Jasper High School really has our house president intrigued!" Everyone loves specific praise, even if it's inaccurate, so I was interested in how many people would show up for the dinner the first time I invested a half-day in making these calls.

We drove to the Beta house at 4:55 on the appointed Monday, and there were at least 150 sport-coat-clad guys milling around the front yard waiting for the doors to open. We never found out how the Betas handled this bounty of potential members, but every September during my time in Bloomington they had the opportunity to enjoy the company of young, eager, easily-duped freshmen whose last names began with A.

My other favorite phone-driven prank was to randomly call students to tell them their names had been drawn in a contest to win a new TV at a Bloomington business. Virtually all of the calls went like this:

"Hello."

"Hi! Is Mike Henke in?"

"This is Mike!"

"Mike, Dave Murphy here from Dave's TV on North Walnut. Your name was drawn in our contest to win a slightly-used 25-inch television. Congratulations!"

"You might have the wrong guy. I don't remember entering a contest for a TV."

"Is this Mike Henke from 1341 Mill Lane in New Albany?"

"Yeah, that's me."

"Then you're the winner. Come on down to the store to pick up your new TV!"

"All right! See you in a little bit!"

I could make 20 of those calls in an hour, and so for the rest of the day people streamed into Dave's TV asking for their TVs.

This is a bit mean-spirited, but I always thought the joke was on the people at Dave's TV who had to endure an entire day — or several days — of breaking bad news to the endless parade of people who walked into the store with an expectation of leaving with a free TV worth in the neighborhood of $500. As much fun as it is to fulfill the wishes of winners, it must be conversely miserable to dash their dream.

For those of you who have grown weary of phone-based silliness — the kind that sadly (for me) ended with the advent of caller ID and smart phones — I'll shelve the rest of my library in favor of one more story that involved a little tech-savvy industriousness.

Back in the 1980s, cable TV was delivered to apartments via a network of coaxial cables that dispersed signals through a common box at each building to each individual apartment. The boxes were supposed to be locked, but given the number of boxes and cable installation people who needed quick access, none of the boxes were locked. This allowed apartment dwellers to manage their own cable independent of the company. Cable piracy in Bloomington was so rampant that no one was prosecuted. It occurred to us one afternoon that not only could cable easily be stolen, we could get in on the distribution end with a VCR and a three-foot long coaxial cable.

Here's how it worked: we rent a VHS copy of *Edward Penishands*, or some other cheap porn flick, and play it on the VCR in Paulie Balst's apartment. We then connect a coaxial cable from the cable jack in the box for Paulie's apartment to the jack for the apartment of four girls we knew.

Back in the low-tech 1980s, remote controls for cable boxes all operated on the same frequency, so my remote would work for every other cable box in Bloomington. When the four girls came home to their apartment, we started the porn and changed their cable box to channel three. Boom! Raunchy porn for girls who wanted to watch *Dynasty*. They were baffled by the programming option that had been chosen for them instead of by them.

They tried to change the channel, and we quickly changed it back to three. They hit the top of the TV, shook the box, and turned the TV off. We turned it back on. They turned it off again, and we waited for a couple of minutes so they would get comfortable and then turned it on. They screamed, and we laughed out loud.

Nothing like free time, and there is no time freer for college students than after a Saturday night tour of campus bars.

A friend of ours graduated at the end of the fall semester and moved home to Chicago. He continued to get mail at the apartment he shared with Paulie, Lou, and Jeff. After a night in the bars, I thought it might be a good idea to go through his mail to make sure he wasn't missing out on an important piece of information.

There was one very nice letter from his friends near his childhood home in Boston. The letter was so touching, Paulie thought it would be nice if I called them as our friend — collect. I told this family I was on my way to visit them. I planned to arrive the next afternoon, and they should "have ham sandwiches and gin & tonics ready!" They seemed excited my friend would be visiting the next day.

It was a fun call, so I did it again two weeks later to explain why I (he) didn't show up — car trouble in Pennsylvania, but I would be there tomorrow (again) come hell or high water, so (again) have the ham sandwiches and gin & tonics ready.

A year went by without us thinking about the calls again. We went to a party where the friend who was supposed to visit his friends attended. He asked if any of us had ever felt we had "lost time." When he described his experience, it sounded vaguely familiar, "I paid a surprise visit to some friends in Massachusetts, and they were really cold to me," he said. "I asked what was wrong, and they told me about calling them twice as I was on my way. They said I told them to have ham sandwiches and gin & tonics ready. That sounded like me, so I must have called."

Paulie and I started laughing. We explained that I made the calls after a couple of nights out. Rather than being angry, the friend was relieved that he wasn't blacking out during long expanses of his life.

It occurred to me that we had totally forgotten about the calls, just as we had so many other practical jokes. It was weird that our friend's question about lost time, deja vu and other psychological phenomena brought this to an organic and unlikely resolution. I couldn't help but wonder how many dopey practical jokes we had forgotten that might have started a butterfly effect in the lives of others.

Lessons learned:

1. When you put into action a practical joke, sometimes the outcome is not exactly what you intended. There is no unringing the bell of a practical joke.

2. As my grades in college weren't tremendous, my time might have been better invested in studying rather than figuring out how to pump porn into the apartment of neighbors.

3. Free time is not my friend. Idle hands are the devil's workshop. Hard work is a key deterrent to inane revelry!

4. If the energy spent to disrupt the lives of strangers was better invested, global warming and world hunger could be solved in a week.

Leaving Harrisburg in a Hurry

After college, I had no idea what I would do next. That's what happens when you graduate with a journalism degree — opportunities are scarce, and good jobs are impossible to get without experience. There was no doubt what I would be good at, but there was also no doubt I was under qualified to an alarming degree for any of those jobs.

Management seemed like fun. The thought of assembling a great team, empowering them, and providing them the resources necessary to succeed always seemed in my wheelhouse — and it would be 20 years later. Being a talent was doable, but I was an acquired taste, so no one would hire me without a track record of success.

My public speaking professor at Indiana kind of nailed it when at the end of the semester she described my performances, "I would never teach anyone to make presentations in the way Kent does, but I won't change a single thing that he does. His quirks make him memorable." I took it as a compliment.

Dad was riding my ass about getting a job, so my motivation wasn't to get a job I wanted, but to stop Dad's noise. I was cooking pizzas at a Little Caesar's a few blocks from my parents' house, and Julie was at her parents' home. We wanted to get married, but there was no way I would get married while being a pizza cook, so that was another motive to find something that somehow validated my educational focus in broadcast journalism.

Toward that end, I called my broadcasting professor at Indiana, the great Richard Yoakam, each week to see if there might be a gig he had heard about for which I was a fit. Professor Yoakam was as good a guy as he was a professor, so he told me about a news photographer position at WSIL-TV in Harrisburg, Illinois — a town in the far southern part of the state. He told me the pay was terrible, but that it was full time and the cost of living in Harrisburg was similar to Ecuador, so it all evened out.

The interview was a mostly useless exercise to make sure I knew which end of the camera to point at what I wanted to shoot. The job was mine, and Yoakam was right — the pay was awful. The general manager/news anchor (yes, the GM was also the anchor of the 5 p.m. and 10 p.m. news) told me the hourly rate was $3.50, and overtime was not allowed. She added that every three months I would receive at 25-cent raise until my pay was capped at $5/hour. I shook her hand, and was told I could start Monday.

My parents were curious about where I might live on an annual salary of $7,280. I told them it was already set. My roommate would be a reporter/anchor named Walt Buteau, and we would live across the street from the station in an apartment above a flower shop so I wouldn't need to buy a car.

Mom and Dad moved me in the next Sunday. The apartment was not what you would call opulent. There was a bedroom, small kitchen, and living room with a Murphy Bed. Mom looked in the refrigerator, and went straight for the Lysol and scrub brush. Layers of mold covered almost every surface. I bumped into the wood paneling and heard a rattling as though something was falling. Turned out the noise was made by displaced cockroach nests. I didn't notice the potholes in front of the building on State Road 13, but despite not needing a car, I became well acquainted with them as coal trucks rolled by 24/7 causing quite a bit of noise.

Mom cried in the car as she and Dad left her media professional in utter squalor, but I was excited about the opportunity. Telling visual stories for the people of southern Illinois, northern Kentucky, and southeastern Missouri might be fun. I barely knew anything about shooting news, so there would be an opportunity to learn how to shoot and edit. As long as I'm learning, I'm happy.

There were successes and failures in Harrisburg. Because of the pay, virtually everyone on WSIL's staff was 22-25. It was kind of an extension of college. We drank a lot of beer, worked as hard as we could, and had a lot of laughs. This was very similar to summer camp, but without being responsible for the lives of a bunch of kids.

We played softball in a townie league, drove to Carbondale (home of Southern Illinois University) on the weekends, and learned to economize.

There were four moments that communicated loudly to me that my destiny was neither in news photography nor southern Illinois. Any of these experiences would have been an overwhelming epiphany for a normal person, but I would not be deterred. Here they are in no particular order:

In the spring, Illinois Secretary of State Jim Edgar spoke at Rend Lake Community College, and I had to shoot some B-roll, the video content that airs over the top of a narration by an anchor. By this point I knew what I was doing, so I knew the shots I needed. Back in 1987, photogs carried both a bulky camera and a large tape deck that was roughly double the size of a VCR. The camera and deck weighed about 10-12 pounds each, and they were connected by a cable. We also carried a stick microphone that was also connected to the deck.

I climbed on stage, got a shot from the side, and another from behind showing the audience. Then I got a little ambitious (by now you know that whenever I write "I got a little ambitious," get ready for something idiotic). I decided to begin a shot of Edgar's profile and then move toward the front of the stage to get him straight on. If I'm going to shoot B-roll, why not make it look unique?

As I moved toward the front of the stage, my left leg became entangled in the cable connecting the camera to the deck and I stumbled. I backpedalled quickly to regain my footing, but before my equilibrium was re-established, I ran out of stage and fell five-feet onto my back. Because I'm a company guy, I did everything necessary to save the equipment. Edgar interrupted his remarks to check on me, and I assured him I was fine.

The camera was rolling as I fell, so the video became a big hit at the station. This was before YouTube, or you would likely have seen it yourself.

A couple of months in, I was assigned a story about a 10-year-old child suffering from cystic fibrosis. Back in the 1980s, CF victims lived into their teens and maybe just a bit beyond, and the treatments were physically withering. Every four hours, a sufferer had to have his or her chest and back beaten with cupped hands to loosen the mucus that gathered in the lungs. We shot that, as well as the girl playing with dolls, crayons, and other normal childlike behavior.

The parents did everything possible to help their daughter, and I tried to shoot it as a lasting testimonial to the bravery of the entire family. It was beautiful, and the reporter on the story knew it. When we got in the car she told me that if I did my job right she would put this story at the very front of her resume' tape. She said I should do the same. In Harrisburg, everyone was working as hard at getting their next job as they were at excelling in their current position, so resume' tapes were frequently discussed.

I stayed silent after the reporter made her incredibly pragmatic and callous comment, but my immediate thought was to get the hell out of Harrisburg and TV news. If my success required using the misery of a kid with CF, I would rather cook pizzas.

The reporter never got the job in a bigger market that she craved. I saw her in a Chicago shopping mall three years later and she was selling real estate.

The third episode that doomed my future in Harrisburg taught me that details — big and small — are vital.

In June, I shot a story at a bank in Harrisburg that gave handguns to anyone who opened a new account at a certain level. This was a funny story that would serve as a kicker on Jimmy Breslin's late night show on ABC, and I shot it well. It was late in the afternoon, and we had a very tight window to get back to the station and edit the package.

Back then, we had bulky cases for the cameras that fit snugly in the hatch of our Nissan Sentra news units. In addition to the camera, we had the tape deck and tripod. Getting all of them in the hatchback was a pain. The reporter asked me about the order of the shots as I loaded the equipment. We jumped into the car, and I slammed it into reverse. As I backed up, it felt like I hit a speed bump. My heart dropped.

Yep, I ran the right rear tire over the camera.

I forgot to put the camera in its case, and ran over the damn thing. We spent a lot of time at the station talking about historic screw ups in TV news, but I never heard one about a photog running over a camera with a news unit.

The reporter joined me behind the car, and I swore her to secrecy as we examined the carnage. Despite my pay being roughly 40% of what it took to get to the poverty level, I didn't want to be fired. Lying is abhorrent to me, but getting the ax wasn't going to magically fix the camera. I told the reporter to head straight to the editing booth when we got back to the station, and I would take care of the story.

Being around my dad taught me that anger can be a tactic to throw people a little off-balance. Dad never did it for that reason. He wasn't being strategic, he was just angry — a lot. I blew into the station hotter than hell, and I yelled that I needed an engineer. When the chief engineer poked his head out of his office, I scowled and walked straight at him holding the camera housing in one hand and the disconnected lens in the other.

"How do you like this shit, Pat!" I yelled. "I'm shooting a goddamned stand-up, and the lens falls right off the damn housing. How are we supposed to do our jobs when the equipment sucks like this. I want this fixed — *now!*"

Pat was totally bamboozled. He looked at the remains of the camera like something didn't compute, and said he would take care of it.

I felt awful for lying. Pat was an exceptionally nice man and deserved better than what I gave him that afternoon.

A few days later, the camera was fixed, and Pat explained his belief that the camera must have been damaged when I fell off the stage in front of a stunned Jim Edgar. I nodded as though I gave it a little thought, and said, "You know, that makes sense." That was the last I heard of the camera being run over by the car.

The final straw occurred in July, after Julie and I married. The general manager/news anchor had promised that 25-cents per hour raise every three months, and she was true to her word the first two quarters. At the nine —month mark, I asked for the bump to $4.25. She claimed never to have made that promise. I argued to no avail, and then grabbed the other full-time photog, who confirmed she had indeed made that promise.

I was furious. Julie and I were somehow getting by on $8,320 per year, and that extra quarter would make a difference. Money was so tight that I perfected getting my blood pressure to measure 120 over 80 so I could win a $25 gift certificate at Kroger for having a "perfect" reading. Hey, $25 was good for 28 frozen Totino's Pizzas!

Julie hated Harrisburg because of the relentless heat and noise from the coal trucks. I didn't allow Julie to apply for a job despite her protests because it might mean settling down in Harrisburg permanently. If she got a job we might have decided to stay, and that was out of the question. We like cities, and places where the temperature drops below 85 at night.

In early August, Julie was offered a job in Chicago. I found that out on Wednesday, August 5th at 11:30 a.m. By 11:45 a.m., I gave notice that I would work through the end of the week and that would be it. The GM/anchor said, "You're giving me two-and-a-half days notice? Only two-and-a-half days?"

I glared at her, and said "Yep."

Lessons learned:

1. Even if your boss is a tool, don't lower yourself to his or her level. I spend no time thinking about my boss in Harrisburg, but regret lying about the camera and giving short notice. It was classless and beneath me.

2. When you get that feeling in your gut for the first time that you are in the wrong place, give a fair notice immediately.

3. Try to make more than what $8,320 in 1987 is worth today when you get married.

4. If the only way to cool your apartment is to open a window 20 feet from a giant pothole in the middle of a coal truck route, pack and leave immediately.

5. When in doubt, all feedback should be welcomed as a compliment.

Welcome to the World — Your Father is a Shoplifter

Julie was two weeks late for her period and thought she might be pregnant. I walked from our studio apartment in Chicago's Old Town to the Walgreens to buy a pregnancy test kit. We had a spare couple of bucks, so it wouldn't be a major investment.

At that point, five months after we were married, money wasn't exactly flowing in. Julie had her job at a small telecommunications firm, and I was a day away from starting my job working as a runner for Chicago Corp. at the Chicago Board Options Exchange.

We lived in an okay place in a good neighborhood right across the street from St. Michael's Church, adjacent to Cabrini Green — one of the most dangerous neighborhoods in America.

Credit card companies called quite often, badgering us to pay some bills. I had run up a balance on our Sears card, and we bought a hide-a-bed from Carson's on credit. Keeping up with payments was impossible, so the calls kept coming.

Money was tight is the point. Really tight. So tight that the spare couple of bucks I referred to in the first paragraph was literally two dollars.

So as I walked the aisles of the Walgreen's, I hoped the kit needed to determine whether Julie was pregnant was somewhere in the $1.50 range. That way, I could pick up a hot dog on the way home. Twenty -five-year-olds have a tendency toward that level of feed-me-now stupidity. At least I did.

The kit's actual retail price was $9.95. If I had been a contestant on "The Price Is Right", Bob Barker would have laughed at my ignorance as I was ushered off the stage a loser.

The packaging of the kit was really thin, so I thought about stuffing it down my pants. Two things crossed my mind in the moment — if I was caught and prosecuted for shoplifting, it would make for a strange but hilarious story; and, there is no chapter about theft in *Dr. Spock's Baby and Childcare.*

Wondering whether Julie was pregnant until we could put together the $10 needed to buy the test was not an option, so down my pants the test went. I walked out of the store consciously thinking about that Sunday's Bears game so the shame of stealing a pregnancy test wasn't written all over my face. I don't know where I learned that helpful lesson of successful larceny, but it worked well enough that I was not arrested.

The result proved Julie knew her body well enough that the test was an unnecessary expense — or, in my case, risk.

Before Julie gave birth to Ryan, I quit my job at the CBOE and started work as a clerk in a video store, Julie's employer went under, our car was stolen, and we moved into a tiny two-bedroom apartment three miles to the north just 11 days prior to Julie giving birth. The four primary selling points of the new place were (1) proximity to Wrigley Field (just six blocks south), (2) proximity to old college friends (right around the corner from Paulie and Larry), (3) the two bedrooms, and (4) the below market rent thanks to a very generous building owner.

These criteria all seemed normal to us, which seems exceptionally odd today. Like you are learning through reading this book, we are learn-as-you-go types of people.

The day Julie went into labor started with another moment that does not qualify as my best. At 5:30 in the morning on June 10th, Julie woke me up and said, "I think it's happening."

"You should go back to sleep. It's probably something else. Better wait a couple of hours to be sure," I told her, because I was exhausted and really wanted to get back to sleep.

Julie is not prone to anger. She is tolerant to a fault — at least with me — but not this time. I was told to wake my ass up, and drive to her parent's house in Griffith, Indiana. Her dad was a physician and her mom a nurse, so we would be in good hands on our way to the hospital, near their home.

Both Dr. And Mrs. Purcell confirmed waking up early had been a good idea, as Julie was in the early stages of labor. We got to the hospital at 3:30 p.m., as the time between contractions lessened and the severity of the pain built.

The doctor popped in occasionally and the nurse was a helpful companion for Julie as I watched the Cubs beat the Cardinals, 7-3, in St. Louis. I would have been happy to help in some small or significant way, but sadly the man is virtually useless during childbirth. I tried to give support to Julie, but she was not shy in expressing her disinterest in my coaching.

As the action in Julie's birth canal became more intense, I became more engaged. I called my parents and Julie was in contact with her's.

We had discussed names a bit during the pregnancy. Julie liked Ryan if we had a boy, and for some reason I limited Ryan to being the name only if he was blond. We had no idea the sex of the baby, so we were covered only if we had a blond boy — a long shot, as we both have brown hair.

The baby, complete with a penis and blond hair, popped free at 1:10 a.m. on June 11th. The nurse cut the umbilical cord, wiped him clean, and handed him to Julie.

"It's Ryan!" Julie cried after the bravest 19 hours and 40 minutes of her life.

Her relentless strength amid the pain and physical exertion of child birth was incredible to watch. It was like watching a powerlifter run a marathon while being beaten with a pineapple.

Ryan opened his eyes, seemed to assess his surroundings, and barely cried. It was like he was born 32 years old. What I hadn't realized is that childbirth is not over after the baby is expelled. There is more work to be done, and I'm not going to get into the episiotomy. (If you don't know what is is and are tempted to look it up, don't!)"

Julie was a radiant gray, if there is such a thing. If lifeforce can be expressed as a percentage, Julie was down to about 2% physically — but 150% spiritually.

Ryan was 20 1/2 inches long, seven pounds, four ounces, and graded well on the Apgar.

My parents and sister had driven up from New Albany, and were thrilled to meet their first grandson and nephew. Everyone was ecstatic all had gone well — or so we thought.

I slept on a cot in Julie's room and awakened at 9:30 later that same morning. I told Julie, "I had the strangest dream. The doctor came in and told us Ryan stopped breathing twice during the night and needed a spinal tap."

Julie's eyes widened. "I had the same dream!"

"Shit!"

I ran across the hall to the nursery, and there was Ryan, the perfect baby, with tubes everywhere. The nurse explained he was born with Sepsis. Sometimes, if the mother's water doesn't break and escape completely, the baby can develop a severe infection that can cause a variety of issues, including death. She told us he had stopped breathing twice, but started again on his own. They quickly administered massive doses of antibiotics, and were confident of a healthy prognosis, which is meaningless to parents looking at a baby — their baby — covered with bandages, tubes, and wires.

The spinal tap would confirm the diagnosis, and Ryan would stay in the hospital for the next 10 days.

I cannot begin to explain the helplessness of having a baby whose life is threatened. It's a radical change to become responsible for a new life that didn't exist the day prior. To watch that baby fight for his life provides an inkling of the emotional reservoir of strength all of us have.

Julie and I were among the lucky ones. Ryan regained his health because the nurses were diligent and reacted immediately during his first few hours, and all restrictions expired as he turned one month old. He was healthy, fine. But we never forgot, and we never took Ryan's health for granted. We celebrated the end of that month by taking Ryan to Wrigley Field to see the Cubs play the Dodgers in a doubleheader.

We carried Ryan the six blocks to the ballpark, and bought two tickets in the upper deck on the third base side. The Cubs were swept 1-0 and 6-3. Ryan slept through both games, showing at a very early age that he was destined to become the smartest Sterling.

I don't know whether this is true for all parents, but Julie instantly became a great mother. I evolved into a solid father after a period of time. My love for Ryan was always uppermost in my mind, but I really didn't figure him out until he began running, talking, and throwing.

At nine months, Ryan ran to the TV during a car commercial to take his first steps. He started shooting baskets at 18 months, and throwing and hitting whiffle balls a year later.

His favorite TV shows were IU and Chicago Bulls basketball, Cubs baseball, and car commercials. If Julie and I watched something else, he left the room.

There is a remarkable switch that flips when you have a child. A life whose most important priority had been his or her own pleasure and validation changes in a second. Protecting this new life consumes you and there will never be another moment when that new life is out of your thoughts.

My being improved by an infinite factor on June 11, 1988, and not because the Cubs won the night before. As much as I tried to teach Ryan, I learned an enormous amount by paying attention to him, and more through watching him always do the right thing as though it was the only choice.

Those who believe their lives end when they have their first child are correct, in a sense. The life led prior to welcoming that new family member ends the moment a baby is born. A new life — a much better and more rewarding existence — replaces it.

Thinking about the man I wanted Ryan to become improved the man I was. Not wanting Ryan to bear the stigma of being the son of a shoplifter, 13 years after I stuffed the pregnancy test down my pants, Julie and I returned to the Chicago Walgreens. I popped in, told the baffled cashier the story of my petty theft, and gave her $10.

She complained there was no precedent for my corrective act and didn't know how to process the payment, so I grabbed a pregnancy test from the same shelf where they were kept in 1987 and had her ring it up. I paid for it, and then returned it to the shelf.

Like any father trying to raise a son with a broad and strong moral base, I settle all accounts.

Lessons learned:

1. Never look at the beginning of what's next as the end of what's been. What's next is usually better — unless it's a tax audit, medical diagnosis, or death (depending upon your religious persuasion).

2. Get out of the delivery room before the episiotomy.

3. Trusting your wife's intuition about pregnancy is wiser than shoplifting.

4. A Cubs doubleheader is no way to introduce your son to all that is outside his four walls — at least it wasn't in 1988.

5. It's never too late to make amends.

Give Us 22 Minutes, We'll Move WMAQ

"Any of you guys know how to drive a truck?" WMAQ station manager Scott Herman asked a group of producers, including me.

This was 1990, and I was in the midst of a three-year immersion into acting and improvisation. One thing I was told again and again and again is if someone asks if you can do something — catch a football, ride a horse, or lift 100 pounds over your head — always say yes, even if you can't.

WMAQ was about to move from its longtime home at Chicago's Merchandise Mart to a brand new NBC Tower three-quarters of a mile away, and Herman needed a guy to drive the truck full of equipment from the Mart to our new home.

I said "Yes," before anyone else, so I was it — the driver, the man entrusted to get behind the wheel with all those computers, files, and furniture. I never asked Herman a question — not how big the truck was or whether I would have to back the truck into a loading dock. Just a big fat juicy "yes."

Herman handed me a slip of paper with the address of the place where I was to pick up the truck the following morning. He told me to drive it to the Mart's garage by 8 a.m, and I assured him I would. Actors who say yes have days or weeks to learn whatever expertise they have claimed to possess. I had 14 hours.

The attendant at the rental place walked me back to where the truck was parked, and I tried to look beyond the 18-wheeler to see the small U-Haul that I thought I would be wrangling through the streets of Chicago for the next two days. I circled around the semi, and there was no truck behind it. "Is this it?" I asked, and the attendant told me it was. I had never driven anything remotely similar to this truck. The closest I had ever been to the inside of a truck this size came when I saw *Smokey & the Bandit* at a drive-in in the late 1970s.

I climbed in, gave the attendant a big thumbs-up, pressed down on the clutch, and turned the ignition. It fired just like the big rig Jerry Reed drove from Atlanta to Texarkana and back in the hit Burt Reynolds flick. I made the stick go to the place corresponding to the R on the little ball on the stick shift, and I backed out.

There are a lot of places and times that might be better to drive a semi for the first time than Chicago during rush hour, but that was my responsibility, so I gave it a shot. The key was to get out of the lot without making the attendant nervous. It helped that I got to the exit of the lot between surges in traffic and merged easily without coming to a complete stop. I gave the guy a wave, and tried not to look like I was aware that I was woefully unprepared for any part of driving that beast in any environment — much less Chicago.

Pulling into the garage at the Mart was easy the first time, because I drove in forward. Producers Mike Greenberg (yes, that Mike Greenberg — the guy who now hosts "Get Up" every morning on ESPN) and Terry Bauer, who's still enjoying a long career in Chicago media, were waiting. Greeney gave me the bad news that to load the truck I would have to back it in, which I did with a level of ease that stunned me.

Countless times over the next two days, we navigated between the two buildings. The drives back to the Mart were slightly less harrowing because the truck was empty, and the only damage that could be done was to the truck (a rental) and to the human cargo — three $8 per hour producers. Backing into the loading dock at NBC Tower was a little nerve-racking, as we only had about a foot clearance on either side as we squeezed in.

We developed a bit of a system with Greeney on one side and Terry on the other signaling which way I needed to correct to position the truck perfectly for loading and emptying the truck.

One uncomfortable but instructive moment during the move occurred in the Mart as Terry and I both carried boxes of garbage. I was a little frustrated that the move wasn't a team activity embraced by upper management, so I said to Terry, "What I want to know is where the hell (general manager) Rick Starr is as we are carrying garbage to the dumpsters?" I felt an odd sense of unease, and looked behind me. Not 20 feet back, there was Rick hauling a bunch of garbage too. Management was right there with us — I just had not seen them.

That was the end of my bitching and whining about management. Despite assumptions by the rank and file, most managers work damn hard — that's how they got to be managers in the first place. When I became a manager, it was of paramount importance that no one on the staff ever correctly invoked my name as someone who didn't pull his weight.

I never hit a thing with the truck, and the move was executed on time and on target. I don't believe anyone suspected that I was full of it when I proclaimed expertise in driving a truck. If they did, they kept their mouths shut.

The new facilities were immaculate. The newsroom looked like the bridge of Star Trek's Starship Enterprise. It felt like we were a part of history as we moved the station into what would be its home for the next half century — at least.

Not quite.

WMAQ lasted another 10 years as a great news station before it was replaced on the frequency by a more profitable sportstalk station. 670 AM has been the home of The Score — Chicago's first (and best) sportstalk — since.

The Score moved from NBC Tower to the Prudential Building another 10 or 11 years later, so all that work is nothing but a memory — and so it goes.

For those who believe because of his performance on ESPN that Greenberg is not the kind of guy who would be much use during a move like this, I can tell you that he pulled his weight and then some. Greeney, Terry, and I will never be mistaken for the burly fellas who normally do that kind of work, but we busted our asses to the point Herman hooked us up with suite tickets to a White Sox game during the final season at old Comiskey Park. When Herman handed us the tickets, he said, "I have only one demand — you don't leave a single beer in the fridge."

We didn't.

I learned another piece of perspective on radio management the next year. Herman had been promoted by Westinghouse (they owned WMAQ at the time) to a position in Philadelphia, and was replaced by Jim Frank, a Chicago news legend. Frank was not the same kind of manager as Herman. Herman had great respect for people at all levels of the station, and made sure they felt appreciated. We received personal notes of encouragement, and on holidays all three shifts were fed well. Frank was not nearly as enamored with the producers.

Greeney was taken off the schedule by Frank — not fired — just parked. I'm not sure why. He had always been a hard-working guy, and Frank's indifference to Greeney defied logic. A fellow former WMAQ staff member was in the process of launching Chicago's first sports talk station, so Greeney went to work there. Within a couple of years, Greeney was hired by ESPN2 and then ESPN Radio.

If Greeney had accepted Frank's appraisal of his work, he leaves radio and gets a real job. If media reports are accurate, he's now earning $6.5 million a year to talk about sports.

In 1990, he (and I) made $8 per hour to cut tape, take audio feeds, change the instacart machine, stuff bumper stickers into envelopes, and help move a great radio station six blocks. We never complained (much), volunteered to do crazy stuff like drive a semi, and understood that a radio station is only as strong as what appear to be its least important people.

Lessons learned:

1. Say yes when asked to do something you have never done — unless it poses the danger of immediate physical harm.

2. Don't bitch about management — instead, understand they got their jobs by doing something at a high level when they were lowly pups at the bottom of the corporate ladder.

3. Pretending to be a master will prepare you to be a master.

Welcome to
Second City

Second City Training Center is a unique facility in Chicago that draws comedy wannabes and truly gifted comedic actors. The list of alums reads like a comedy hall of fame — Bill Murray, Tina Fey, Steve Carell, Joan Rivers, John Belushi, Amy Poehler, Mike Nichols, Elaine May, Stephen Colbert, Jane Lynch, Chris Farley, Bonnie Hunt, Adam McKay, and many more. Its method of teaching improvisational comedy is revered.

Living in Chicago in 1990, I thought taking classes at Second City would be both frightening and fun. I knew nothing about improv — other than I loved watching it done by those who were really good at it. Unfortunately, Second City's standards did not allow for rogue kooks without any theatrical background to walk in off the street to enjoy instruction in the art of making people laugh with their wits, and only their wits.

The people at Second City recommended a class for beginners at a place called The Players Workshop of Second City. In my mind there was no difference between the two, so I walked into Players Workshop, wrote a check for $150, and was welcomed into an eight-week session of three-hour classes each Wednesday.

The first Wednesday night, I walked into the building scared shitless. I knew no one in the class, knew nothing about acting or improv, and was quite certain I would fail. But I also had a great sense of excitement. This was the behavioral equivalent of jumping off a cliff. I was certain the end would be hideous, but the fall might be exhilarating.

Like anyone without any idea how difficult improv is, I wanted to jump straight in during the first class, hop on stage, and engage in hilarious banter. Just like facing a major league fastball should not be the first exposure a baseball player gets to hitting, introductory instruction in improv required we walk before running. The first few classes involved games developed by a woman named Viola Spolin. You've likely never heard of her, but everyone who delves into improv becomes very aware of her methods. As this is not a book on improv, I will simply explain these classes as exercises in paying attention to one another rather than being focused on yourself.

There were six eight-week modules, and I improved to the point where I felt quite comfortable jumping onstage with almost any classmate. Prior to one class late in the process, the instructor, (a good dude named Doug), asked me to follow him out of the building. I thought perhaps my latest check had bounced or I was being tossed from class. His message was quite different — I was good enough to audition for Second City's Touring Company in his opinion, which was very nice to hear.

I didn't heed his advice, as I was damn certain I was not ready to be paid to improvise. The classes continued, and I believed that maybe I wasn't wasting my money — not because I was the next Bill Murray, but because improv and talk radio have a great deal in common. Even if I never made anyone laugh from a stage, the experience would translate to talk radio management or hosting. See, I'm not always a stone cold moron!

To try to get some perspective on improv from those who do it best, and because I have a fondness for a great hole-in-the-wall bar, I spent a Wednesday night at U.S. Blues, a spot that was 1/2 block south of Second City on Wells Street. The place was owned in part by Dan Aykroyd and run by Steve Beshekas, an old friend of John Belushi's. I had met Beshekas a couple of times previously, and that Wednesday he introduced me to a Second City actor named Chris Farley.

Farley and I had a great conversation over several beers about Bill Murray, who was Farley's hero, and improvisational genius. Farley was a great guy — funny and sweet.

A couple of weeks later, I saw him again at U.S. Blues. Earlier that night he had been told he would be a part of the new cast of Saturday Night Live, the dream gig for all actors at Second City. I witnessed a different Farley that evening. He sprinted back and forth between the bar and back room. At the bar, Farley knocked back shots of tequila. What he did in the backroom, I don't know. I never went back to find out. Farley mercilessly ridiculed fellow Second City cast members from the bar. I didn't want to be around such mean-spirited energy, and went home. Seven years later, Farley died of a heroin overdose. He was a funny and troubled man.

The year of classes ended with a grad show from the main stage at Second City, which to extend my baseball metaphor was very much like playing a ball game at Wrigley Field or Fenway Park. The seats were filled with friends and family, so they were generous with their laughter.

I had a nice scene with Denny and Tracy that was entirely silent, and it worked really well. Denny and Tracy were seated in front of me as though we were in a movie theater. As they became more amorous, I become involved in their activities without them being aware. It came out of a purely improvised scene during class that we only had to tweak, so it was cool to be in a scene on stage that sprang organically from a few inspired choices by the three of us in class.

Because I graduated from Players Workshop, I was now eligible for classes at Second City. The majority of my classmates from Players Workshop decided enough was enough. Most worked in advertising agencies, and the firm would pick up the tab because developing improv skill improved an employee's job performance.

Second City brought another year of classes and laughs, but it wasn't the pure fun that we enjoyed at Players Workshop. This environment was slightly more cut —throat as my classmates were actual actors. These weren't daytime ad agency types who were willing to let some goofy radio guy take over a scene. They were insecure actors who wanted to feed themselves by catching the eye of an instructor or director.

Some became friends, some didn't.

Ad hoc groups that booked themselves at clubs and bars were formed, and I was invited to join most of them. It was fun, but there was no clear path to fame, fortune, or even solvency. We had a paying gig at a military base south of Chicago and another at a gay bar in Wisconsin. At both, we improvised loudly as we discovered that loud got laughs even if we weren't funny. Quiet and soft is no way to act in a bar whether you're on stage or just drinking.

I learned from the real actors that the job requires an ability to do everything — sing, dance, move, *and* act. Even if you were a master of one thing, you needed to be good at everything else — at least good enough to fake it. Toward that end, I auditioned for a Second City Children's Theatre show. Yes, Second City has (or had) a children's theatre. The rent has to be paid, and kids staring at actors is every bit as lucrative as with adults.

During the audition, we had to sing a one-minute portion of a song, so I picked "Everyday" by Buddy Holly. Singing in public was terrifying to me, especially in front of three or four people who were keenly focused on judging me. I made it through, and one of the people on the panel asked, "Can you sing opera?" I had no idea. Never even tried it alone in the car.

I said, "Sure! What would you like to hear?" There were two possibilities as to what would happen next. Either I would miraculously succeed or I would fail gloriously. Either way was fine with me, and even if I screwed the pooch, lying about whether I could sing opera would not be held against me. Claiming an operatic ability wasn't really a lie because I had no idea whether I could or not. It was a hope. The song that was requested was "Happy Birthday."

My mouth opened, noise came out, and the panel smiled. Again, loud counts, and I was singing very loudly. I gestured like Pavarotti, sang with a vibrato that shocked me, and found a way to continue despite thinking all this very funny. I got the part.

The children's theatre play was a collection of mini-musicals, and I was cast as Little Red Riding Hood's dad in an operatic version of the kids' story. There was no script, so I would make up the melody and lyrics each week as I lamented my daughter being lost in the woods. The kids seemed amused by everything, but the parents were bored out of their minds. I played to them with inoffensive innuendo, and because the show was staged every Sunday during the fall at 1p.m., the Bears were usually playing. A lot of dads were missing the game to culture-up their kids, so I would stuff an update of the score of the game into my little aria.

There was another audition for the Second City Touring Company, and I thought if not now, when? So I called, made an appointment, and waited. On a rainy Tuesday, I showed up with roughly 100 other actors eager to score the lowest paying full-time acting gig in Chicago.

The director told us what was expected — three entrances as different characters asking an information booth attendant how to get to the jewelry store. Easy enough.

There is one major rule in improv. Always be in agreement with the reality of the scene. Never deny an initiation. Guessing what happened next is not hard.

I entered and asked where the jewelry store is. The woman playing the attendant gave me an answer. I said, as though I was trying my best to tank the audition, "Not that jewelry store. I'm looking for Harry Winston." She looked at me like I was clinically insane and told me to go the opposite direction.

I walked backstage, and considered punting on the final two entrances. There is an exit from backstage straight to Wells Street, and I thought heading that way might be a better option than gutting out the next two entrances.

My choice to finish was not fueled by a need to complete the task, but because if I left, the confusion might cause a delay in the auditions. People might just believe I disappeared — *poof!* It would have been unprecedented, and I wish I had bailed if only because I would be *that* guy. They would have asked, "Remember the nut who asked about the jewelry store and then we never saw him again?" That's a better legacy that most who sleepwalk through an audition.

After leaving, I thought, *Okay, more than two years of working my ass off to learn how to do this crap, and I deny an initiation during the audition?* It wasn't fair. So I called a couple of actors with whom I had worked, and was told they got a callback. That gave me an idea — call Second City, and claim a message from them had been garbled on my machine (this was before smartphones, and people actually had a small box that recorded voicemails). They might assume I had been one of the callbacks. That's exactly what happened. I earned a call back through a lie, but what is acting but telling lies in a way that others believe to be true?

The call back had a different format. We were each given scripts and were assigned a partner. The scene I was assigned was an all-time great written during the 1970s. It was right in my wheelhouse as a smart ass husband, and the woman I was paired with was excellent. Finally, I might have been dealt a very good hand.

We were about 30 seconds into the scene when Bob Odenkirk, one of the directors, stopped us. No one outside Chicago knew Odenkirk then, but today we know him as David Cross's partner in *Mr. Show* and as Saul Goodman in *Breaking Bad* and *Better Call Saul*. Bob probably had some good ideas for me, but as I lapsed into a psychotic break, all I did was interrupt him by repeatedly saying, "I got it. Okay. I got it. Uh-huh. Okay." My brain was telling my mouth to shut, but that quiet I demanded of myself never came. I knew immediately that I would be DQ'ed by interrupting Odenkirk, but I just couldn't stop me.

I continued to improvise, and got some positive reviews. Even in shows that were panned, I got good notices. Still, I knew there was some missing chip in my brain that would not allow me to succeed. One night in a scene with a good actor named Bo Blackburn, my mind wandered. This was another night away from my wife and son in order to gain what? Before the scene ended, I knew it was my last. One thing I've always been good at is knowing when to leave.

Any improvisation beyond that would be both futile and self-indulgent, but what I had gained in those three years was a keen understanding of the psychology of performance, and what radio performers need to do their best work. Radio and improv are high-wire acts that require incredible concentration, listening skills, and an abandonment of judgment.

I never worked at Saturday Night Live or became a household name, but the lessons of Second City have helped those with whom I've worked become very successful.

Lessons learned:

1. Don't argue with your internal compass. Mine screamed at me — twice — that my path would not lead to theatrical success.

2. Paying attention to others is more productive than living inside your own head.

3. If it scares you, do it!

Welcome to Cafe Dah-mer-ico, May I Take Your Order?

"What kind of an asshole are you?" the voice on the other end of the phone asked. I had no idea who the voice belonged to, but he sure was angry for a Tuesday at 10 a.m. I've been called an asshole a few times, but never with this level of unbridled fury.

"Who is this?" I asked, sounding a little like Jerry Seinfeld when an angry George Costanza called him.

The caller identified himself as the publisher of a free newspaper in the Lincoln Park neighborhood of Chicago. We had spoken once before. I granted him access to what I published in The Twisted Gazette — a weekly newsletter I wrote and distributed in Chicago's Lincoln Park bars.

I wrote eight pages each week, with stories about our adventures on nights out, critiques of local TV and radio, and stories about local bars. The point was to write things that no one took seriously. No politics, current affairs, or whining. It was all fluff, with a heaping dose of anti-societal detachment.

The publisher of the newspaper was alerted to The Twisted Gazette by a clerk at a Kinko's on Lincoln Avenue where I ran copies. The clerk passed along my phone number. He called offering praise, and I was a big sucker for praise.

He thought my writing was funny and asked if he could print a few things that he liked. Because I'm a sap, I agreed without asking for a little cash in return. There was nothing for me to gain, but I thought I had nothing to lose, so what the hell? More readers seemed better for branding, so our agreement was cemented during that initial phone call. Take what you like — enjoy!

The first and last piece of mine he published was a menu for a restaurant called Cafe Dah-mer-ico. This was a week or two after the sentencing of serial killer Jeffrey Dahmer, the Wisconsin man who killed and ate more than a dozen men in his Milwaukee apartment. The menu was a childish but nicely formatted list of human body parts prepared in a variety of ways, like spleen au gratin topped with pumiced corn and breaded nostrils, or a bowl of toe-mato soup and a grilled cheek sandwich.

There were 12 specific dishes with sides and beverages similarly themed. It was a page filler that was fun to write. The Twisted Gazette dropped every Thursday at about 6 p.m., and people found the menu disgusting but funny, like a Mad Magazine entry.

I never got a call from the guy alerting me to what he grabbed to print in his newspaper. In addition to the menu, he printed a parody movie ad for *Boyz w the Wood* (a barely funny play on *Boyz n the Hood*), but that wasn't what caused the phone call that dissolved our relationship.

The problem was in the menu, the publisher explained. "You must have known, just by the Cafe Dah-mer-ico name. It's just too close." I assured the incensed publishing entrepreneur I had no idea what he was talking about. He continued for minutes on end without any discernible explanation for what caused his angst.

The guy continued yelling without getting to the point, and even then I had a limit for the tonnage of crap I was willing to eat, so I interrupted him. "Look, either explain what the hell you're talking about, or we're done here."

The publisher calmed down and finally shared the improbable source of his rage. He had received a call that morning from the owner of Cafe Ba-ba-reeba, a Lincoln Park restaurant at 2024 North Halsted that still exists today. It was among the many places where his free paper was distributed.

The man was quite distraught about the menu of a restaurant that had a vaguely similar name. I interrupted, "How sensitive is this guy? For God's sake, I'm not implying he is serving tapas with human body parts!"

The publisher was quiet for a couple of seconds, then finally got to the nut of the issue. "The owner's son was one of Jeffrey Dahmer's victims," he said solemnly.

"Oh."

My God. The odds of such a thing happening had to be Power Ball-esque, right? As indifferent to the comedic tastes of blubbering Chicagoans as I was, I certainly had no interest in ripping open the emotional stitches of a father whose son died and was eaten by the creepiest psychopath of the last half century at least.

I assured the publisher I was not the kind of cruel prick who would ever purposefully taunt anyone in that situation, and that this was a horrible coincidence. Then I told him I did not want him controlling the distribution of my work at his whim any longer — as though that made any difference. I knew the owners of most of the bars where The Twisted Gazette was available, and if I mocked them I preferred they knew I meant it.

For many years I had been cavalier about holding people accountable for their stupidity, and gleefully chronicled their exploits. I mocked them with impunity because they deserved it, I felt. But this was different. This was a guy trying to process the worst nightmare a parent could possibly imagine. It's actually beyond what any parent could imagine. I mean, a son being murdered is bad enough without the indignity of being cannibalized.

Like I wrote at the beginning of this chapter, I've been called an asshole before — my 20s were particularly fertile in this area — but I had never actually felt like one. Until that phone call, I had rationalized my way out of a lot of indifference toward the feelings of others with the only goal being a couple of laughs.

It's ironic that the one instance I felt like an asshole was one of the few times I had no intent whatsoever to mock anyone — other than Dahmer, of course. And, obviously, I felt very comfortable that he deserved all the sarcasm that could be thrown in his direction.

I would have liked to apologize to the owner of Cafe Ba-ba-reeba, but how the hell does a person confront a man who lost his son to a cannibal serial killer and apologize for unintentionally making light of his loss? It's futile, impossible, and self-indulgent to apologize only to make me feel better, and I didn't want to insult him further with my feeble effort, so I punted.

Cafe Dah-mer-ico was easy comedy presented with a steaming pile of bad luck. It happens.

Lessons learned:

1. Don't mock people.

2. If you can't curb the impulse to make people laugh through mockery, know it's damn likely you'll ruin a few people's days along the way.

3. Real life cannibals aren't funny.

4. Don't cede power to publish your work for free to someone else — ever. That had nothing to do with my problem here, but it's a good lesson regardless.

Striking Out with the Family

On the second ball of the 10th frame, Dad almost missed the pocket but got a couple of nice taps to rack up his 11th straight strike. As usually happens at a bowling alley when someone strings together a bunch of strikes, a crowd gathered for his 12th ball. Dad didn't bury his final ball deep in the pocket, but it was good enough to get all 10 pins to fall. People cheered, and Dad beamed. It was the only 300 game he ever rolled.

Dad was a good bowler who was exceptionally entertaining. There was never any doubt whether Dad was happy or angry, and he was always happy or angry. When Dad was happy, he was funny, and when he was mad it was hilarious (unless he was mad at you). Dad had competitive charisma that made him really fun to watch. Dad would yell, shriek, bounce, and cavort every week at Bertrand Lanes in Waukegan. As Dad pulled the 16-pound ball from his bag, he would bounce it on the floor to announce his presence. The loud thwump startled everyone in the building.

Mom was — and is — a graceful and athletic bowler, who is still capable of cracking 200 on occasion. She is very competitive, but never shows what she's thinking. Dad wanted to amuse or appall, and always succeeded. As a bowler, I'm a lot more like my dad than my mom — at least in behavior. I never bowled enough to get good at it, but by watching Dad I became well-versed in the misbehavior I found hilarious as a kid.

It's important that I share the bowling history of my family, because the following story makes me sound like a bit of a lunatic if you don't know my dad. I inherited my mom's competitiveness and my dad's lack of shame in causing a commotion in a bowling alley.

My wife, son, and I have bowled together twice. After each excursion, Julie has sworn never to bowl as a family again. The second promise was evidently made in earnest, and I can't blame her.

Our first foray to the lanes was to Waveland Bowl in Chicago on a Sunday. Ryan was four, and we wanted to do something fun as a family. As always, my motives were good and pure, but there are environments where my execution is not quite what I would like. Bowling alleys top the list of those places. People who did not grow up around my dad are not conditioned to expect chaos at the lanes, and they are usually confused or offended.

There is a right way and a wrong way to bowl. For example, gutter protectors should never be deployed for a bowler. Regardless of whether a bowler is four, 14, or 40, it is never acceptable to artificially inflate your score through such contrivances. Ryan was four at the time, and gutter protectors were not going to be part of his first experience as a bowler. Whether or not they would have made the experience more fun was immaterial. There is right and there is wrong. We were going to bowl right.

As usual, my expectations as a bowler were not mirrored by reality. Regardless of the sport, I assume every ball I roll, hit, or throw will go exactly where I picture it in my imagination. My athleticism in my mind's eye is always perfect, and each time I fail to re-create what I envisioned, I get salty. Sometimes, it becomes a self-fulfilling prophecy, and the slide from competent to meltdown is quick — or it used to be. I have adjusted my expectations to a more reasonable level. I remain somewhat volatile, but not at the Clark Sterling 11 on a scale from 1-to-10 level.

But this was 1992, not 2019, so I was at my entertaining best. I whiffed on picking up an easy spare and tried to kick my shoe in a way that it would launch straight up into a ceiling tile. The shoe was a little too tight, so my kick looked more like an Elaine Benes dance move than an attempt to send my shoe skyward like a leather Saturn rocket. Julie gave me a confused "what is that boob doing" look, which steeled my resolve for my next disappointing frame.

Two frames later, I was in a similar situation having left a lone six pin. After missing the spare attempt, I corrected the error from my first effort by nudging the right heel free from the shoe. With the shoe dangling from the rest of my foot, I was ready to launch. I took a step, kicked, and off came the shoe at a speed that even stunned me. And the launch angle was low — as in North Korean missile low. Instead of flying into the ceiling, it rocketed parallel to the ground in the opposite direction of the pins barely missing Ryan's head. It continued through bowlers standing at the counter, whizzed by the cashier's head, and slapped sole first into the paneling behind her. The sound of the shoe hitting the wall was loud enough to distract anyone within 50 feet, so the place went suddenly silent.

As I was the only bowler in the establishment with a single shoe, it would not have taken a trained detective to figure out who was responsible for the projectile that almost decapitated three people (or at least raised a nasty bruise). I had to retrieve the shoe.

At this moment, I had a *Caddyshack*-driven epiphany. I remembered Judge Smails throwing his putter from a green where he had missed a putt into the patio area, where it knocked a female Bushwood member unconscious. He retrieved the putter and blamed his caddy for not pointing out a well worn grip as the elderly lady lay motionless. Having Smails as a role model, even for a brief moment, showed how far afield my conduct had wandered. I stormed toward the cashier, went behind the counter, picked up my shoe, and yelled toward the customers, "Can you believe this? Absolutely ridiculous! Defective shoe! I need some talc! Excuse me — *where is the talc?*"

The cashier was wide-eyed as I spouted nonsense that had nothing to do with the actual cause of the flying shoe. I put the shoe back on and returned to our lane. Julie was having none of my shenanigans. Now and again Julie comes to the realization she married an idiot, and this was one of the those times. This was not funny to Julie — not at all. Ryan was oblivious, which made me feel a little bit better. At least this bizarre episode wasn't going to scar him emotionally. I promised Julie this wouldn't happen again, which seemed a safe bet. While I might indulge in sitcom-esque ill-tempered outbursts once in a while, I was pretty good at not repeating my hijinks.

We bowled again the following year after moving to Indianapolis. I reiterated my vow to bowl without launching a shoe, and we went to the counter to get our shoes and lane assignment. The cashier asked, "Do you want to pay by the game or the hour?" I sensed an opportunity to utilize my penchant for efficiency and shave some money off the cost. After paying for an hour, I told Julie and Ryan we would have to be ready bowlers. If we timed our release correctly, we could get ourselves a free game.

Dad would have been onboard with this, and our family would have complied with his demands to speed bowl. What I always forget about Dad's exploits is that my sister usually yelled at him, and mom would cry.

After a couple of balls, I had the timing of the little gate that sweeps pins down cold, and told Julie and Ryan exactly when to go in order to have the gate rise as the ball approached the pins. This made Julie incredibly nervous, but I was more focused on the drive to squeeze a third game into our hour than Julie's enjoyment. Ryan was even a little shaken by the frenzied pace as I yelled "Ready, *go!*" at perfect intervals.

After seven or eight frames into Game 1, I realized this was not even fun for me. But I was pot-committed to the process, and not going to pay for a second hour. A fun afternoon became a contentious and miserable experience for all of us. Julie muttered several times, "This is not fun." Then she stated clearly, "This is the worst." Finally, she looked me in the eye, and said, "We're never bowling together again."

There have been times since when we have bowled with others, but after the speed bowling debacle the three of us have never gone to a bowling alley a third time. There's a part of me that regrets that, but then again, what the hell, it's only bowling. If you're going to screw up one family activity, bowling is a very dispensable option.

Lessons learned:

1. Be a happy bowler, because in the end, who cares?

2. Happy wife, happy life. Don't anger the little woman over bowling excellence or efficiency.

3. Don't throw or kick things. After they leave your hand or foot, there is no controlling them.

4. Speed of play is fine in moderation.

Hoosier Homecoming

My wife, son, and I were in the car driving back home to Chicago from Indianapolis where a couple of friends spent the weekend trying to talk us into moving to Indy. I thought the suggestion was ridiculous. Who would leave the Windy City for the Circle City? On the surface, it seemed insane.

Then I started silently checking boxes and comparing the two cities. I knew Julie felt little in the way of a tether to Chicago, and I started to see the advantage ebbing toward a place most Chicagoans scoffed at. As is the case in most cities, Chicagoans are very proud. They think of other Midwestern cities as inferior and quaint.

Prospects in Chicago radio were thin, and the writing I was doing in the Twisted Gazette was well-received only by a few hundred troubled malcontents. My weekly newsletter cost more to print that it generated. I'm no genius, but it seemed a good idea that if I was going to write professionally, it was important that I earn more than I spend. Hobbies are usually cash —neutral endeavors. Other than *mistake*, I have no word or phrase for cash —negative operations. Given that this book is about mistakes, that seems appropriate.

I spent time — and money — improvising for three years, and learned a lot doing it. The primary lesson was that I was not good enough at it to get rich. Bill Murray, I was not.

Being a professional actor requires love of the craft, diligence in character development and a brilliance in execution that I lacked. It was fun, but those who succeed at it will tell you earning a living is almost impossible for all but the best, who also happen to be the luckiest.

So what, I asked myself, made Chicago this amazing place that I refused to consider leaving? The answer came to me 20 miles north of Indianapolis. Nothing. Ryan would start school in six months, and our neighborhood in Chicago was a little bit funky, so the school might not put him in the best position to succeed.

I asked Julie if it was all right if I stopped and picked up a Sunday *Indianapolis Star* so we could get a read on area apartments. I got an enthusiastic yes.

We asked Ryan, who was four at the time, whether he would like to move to Indianapolis. He was good with it, too. We always made Ryan a part of decisions. Even though he was four, he was a pretty smart kid. It sounds absurd, but if he had said no, my perspective would have changed.

By the time we got back to our apartment, six blocks south of Wrigley Field, we decided that if I could get a job in Indianapolis, we would pull the trigger.

I called a former co-worker of mine at WMAQ Radio and asked what he knew about Indianapolis radio. He told me there was only one talk station in town, WIBC, and the contact he recommended was Sharon Alseth. I called Sharon to ask if WIBC had any openings, and she referred me to Dan McNeil, the executive producer.

Within an hour, I booked an interview with Dan for a position as a guest booker. All they wanted the person in this position to do was get people on the phone for the two talk shows they produced after morning drive.

I don't toot my own horn about much, but getting difficult-to-reach people on the phone was something at which I was uniquely good.

As a sophomore in college, laying around a friend's room on a Saturday afternoon with a bunch of friends, we thumbed through his endless supply of Playboy magazines. This was before the internet, and Playboys provided a unique opportunity to peruse unclothed women and ponder the possibilities. It sounds crass now, but back then it felt quite evolved. Oh, Playboy also had articles.

On the cover of the latest edition was a picture of Mariel Hemingway, who starred in *Personal Best*, a film about a female athlete who falls in love with a female teammate. Not a bad idea for a film, especially to a bunch of college guys passing idle time on a Saturday thumbing through sofn-porn periodicals.

I said, "Bet you I can get Mariel Hemingway on the phone in less than an hour." The rabble strongly disagreed, but as none of us had any discretionary cash, the wager was joined without stakes.

Again, this was before the internet, so leg work was required to narrow the search. I knew that the Hemingways had a compound in Ketchum, Idaho, where Mariel's grandfather Ernest Hemingway settled, so I called directory assistance (do they even have that anymore?) and asked for the number of a "Mr. Hemingway." The operator said she had three listings, and she was nice enough to violate policy by giving me all three numbers.

The person who answered the first of the three hung up when I asked for Mariel, but the lady who answered at the second number said, "She's not in right now. Can I ask what this is about?" I told the person I wanted to discuss a project with her. She asked my name, and without thinking I said, "Robbie Benson."

Why Benson? No idea. He was an actor at the time, and it felt plausible that he would call. The lady said I should call back in 30 minutes, which is exactly what I did. She said that she had spoken to Mariel and had been directed to share her number with me. I called the number, and Mariel answered. I asked an idiotic question about training for *Personal Best*, and Mariel became agitated. She asked me to write my question down and mail it to her.

I didn't really care about training for a movie. My goal had been accomplished. Inside an hour, I got Playboy's cover girl on the phone.

The point is, communicating with people was not as simple as it is today, and I was good at it. I can't remember whether I related that story to Dan, or just groveled for the gig. Maybe both.

McNeil offered me the job at $5 per hour for 29 hours a week — just under the threshold for a full-time job. I was working at WIBC five days later.

The position gave me a chance to advance quickly, because I was the only person doing it. They hired me into a category I alone occupied. That made it easier for me to excel and be seen as someone who was capable of excellence, even if the only measure was by who I could get to pick up a phone and agree to an interview.

In three months, I earned a dollar-an-hour raise and my hours expanded to full-time. In another 10 months, McNeil quit, and I got the executive producer job with a salary of $22,000 per year — not enough to brag about, but in 1994 radio it was a decent amount.

There is something very empowering about making an amount of money you don't mind walking away from. A couple of months after I got the job, management decided we needed a daily benchmark to drive talk on the street and build ratings. They decided *Confessions Month* was exactly the device to do it.

WIBC was a friendly neighbor talk station with a history of not ruffling feathers. I was told to book sexual deviants as guests for the series. Not knowing any deviants personally, I put personal ads in a few urban newsweeklies, asking for "men and women with atypical sexual appetites willing to share their stories".

In two days, I had *Confessions Month* completely booked. I found an exhibitionist in San Francisco who lived adjacent to an expressway off-ramp. She would stand nude in the window to distract drivers of expensive cars and cause accidents. I found a nude housekeeper, who, well, you get the idea. I also called GG Allin, who was a rock singer with a unique hook. What Gigi did on stage you can google.

After six days, there was talk on the street — *lots* of talk on the street — op-eds in the newspaper, and hundreds of calls from elderly listeners who thought either they were insane or the management at WIBC had lost its mind.

As I drove to work on June 7th, I heard the program director and general manager on the morning show explaining that the idea had been sound but the execution was not what they had asked for.

Uh-oh. I knew what that meant — I was their scapegoat. I parked, walked into the building, found the program director, and with the confidence of a guy making $5 per hour, calmly explained that what had shared on the morning show was nonsense. If anything, I had been restrained compared to what I had been directed to do. Under no circumstance was I going to be the fall guy.

Employees making $5 per hour don't have to take that kind of crap, so I didn't. The next day, I got a raise and full-time status.

I spent the next 17 years working at WIBC and then 1070 the Fan, and my family fell in love with a very underrated town we will always call home.

Two other quick stories about getting people on the phone.

On April, 19, 1995, a lunatic named Timothy McVeigh parked a truck rigged as a bomb in front of the Murrah Federal Building in Oklahoma City. It exploded and killed 168 people. Steve Simpson anchored our coverage and I needed to get someone on the phone who was in the building at the time of the blast.

I asked myself where I would go if that happened in a building where I worked. The answer — a bar. Knowing most bars aren't open in the morning, particularly in a city where buildings had exploded, I called a Hyatt Hotel in downtown OKC because Hyatts always have bars in their atriums. I asked to be transferred to the bar, and asked a bartender if anyone there had been in the Murrah Building. He said there was one guy who had, and handed him the phone. The guy said he would consent to an interview.

This was two hours after the explosion, and to my knowledge he was the first person from inside the building who was interviewed on any media outlet. His description of the chaos and carnage was riveting. Our coverage was unrivaled locally or nationally.

The other story is from when comedian George Burns died in March of 1996. I was asked to get some of Burns' old friends on to reminisce about the late comic. I thought Milton Berle would be a good get, so I thought, "If I were Berle, where would I be?"

Only one place popped into my head — the Los Angeles Friars Club. Directory Assistance gave me the number, and I called.

"Hello, Friars Club."

(in an angry and gravely voice) "Milton Berle!"

"Just a moment." (Maybe a minute passed)

"Hello, Milton Berle here."

"Mr. Berle?"

"Yeah!"

"I'd love for you to join our afternoon show to talk about George Burns."

"Who is this?"

"Kent Sterling from WIBC in Indianapolis."

"How'd you know I was here?"

"Where else would you be?"

"Kid, I'm in the middle of a very important meeting."

"I love your work, and we would only take a couple of minutes."

"Kid, I love you, but we're getting ready to launch a magazine, and this is a very important meeting."

"You're the funniest person I've ever seen — frankly funnier than George Burns, and it will only take a minute!"

"I love you too, kid! Goodbye."

We never got Berle on the show, but guessing where he would be on the first call, and pestering him for a minute was kind of thrilling.

As long as I'm feeling nostalgic, here's one more story. There had been a horrifying disappearance and murder of a kid from Cloverdale named Zachary Snider that WIBC was all over. Out of our coverage "Zachary's Law" was born. It established a sexual predator registry, and remains a great source of pride for those who worked at the station during that time. It's also a very effective tool to keep sexual predators off the street.

Because we were so identified with Zachary's story, we were keen to follow other stories of missing kids, and one morning we saw a report that a child had gone missing the night before. I went to the Criss-Cross directory where media types find phone numbers, names, and addresses if we have any of the other pieces of information. The parents of the kid didn't have a phone, so I grabbed a cell phone and drove to the address listed in the book.

My goal was to get the mother or father of the missing kid on one of our shows. Getting a parent on would humanize the story, publicize the missing kid, and give us a shot at a great segment. I know that sounds a little callous, but that's the job. As I walked up to the house, a Marion County police car pulled up, and a deputy got out. He walked toward the house, smiled at me (so I inferred the news was good) and I called the studio. I told the producer to put me on. The host introduced me, and I held the phone so the deputy was talking directly into it.

"Your son was found this morning in the box car of a freight train in West Lafayette, and he's just fine," the deputy said. The mom and other family members screamed with joy and relief. I handed the phone to the mom, and the next 10 minutes of radio were the best I ever heard.

Lessons learned:

1. City snobbery is ridiculous. All cities aren't the same, but most have their good points. We got lucky that Indianapolis was a good town when we got here. It's only improved since.

2. Being a big fish in a small pond instead of a small fish in a big pond is better for building a career.

3. Milton Berle must have spent a lot of time at the Friars Club.

4. Taking a shot in the dark — whether in a move to another city, getting a celebrity on the phone, or being at the front door of a terrified mother — sometimes pays dividends. Never allow the potential fruitlessness of an enterprise discourage you from taking a shot.

Pontificating from the Cheap Seats to Get the Colts

Shortly after Emmis Communications acquired WIBC Radio, there was a meeting in an Indianapolis hotel conference room where a recent research project was discussed. You won't be surprised to learn I stepped way out of line.

Radio stations conduct surveys and commission research projects from time to time to determine which hosts, music, and format ideas work — and which don't. This meeting was a great opportunity for Emmis Communications big wigs like CEO Jeff Smulyan to get a snapshot of his property and employees.

The meeting revealed many areas of growth and concern, and all were discussed. I was the executive producer at the time, so my input was not required. I kept my mouth shut and listened to everyone else. My strategy was to keep my opinions to myself until the program director and I were alone. That way, I could provide input without openly disagreeing with my direct report or causing a problem with upper management.

At this point I had not enjoyed the opportunity to spend significant time with Smulyan. I grew to respect him and consider him a friend, but at this point he was about six levels above my pay grade, so being silent made all kinds of sense.

The conversation turned from the research study to the question of how serious WIBC should be about acquiring the play-by-play rights to Indianapolis Colts football games. Three years prior, WIBC had lost the rights to rivals WNDE and Q95, and it hindered the station's ability to build listenership.

Our GM, Tom Severino, explained to Smulyan where he stood in the negotiations with the Colts. Both sides had agreed upon a three-year deal, but the Colts wanted an extra $100,000 per year and Severino was not enthusiastic about committing additional cash to the deal.

Smulyan asked our program director for his thoughts, and he fell in line with Severino. Next up was our promotions director, and he fell in line with Severino too.

While they talked, I pondered what I would say if Smulyan asked for my opinion. My opinion was far bolder than the others. I stridently supported spending the cash. You want to make an omelette, you break eggs. My passionate internal monologue spoke to the need to be bold, assert to listeners and local radio companies that WIBC as owned by Emmis would be different — fearless, daring, and courageous.

Lost in my thoughts, I barely heard Smulyan when he actually did ask what I thought. Only his eye contact communicated to me that it was my turn. Instantly, I decided that if the CEO asked for my opinion, by God, he would get my opinion.

I ranted for 10 minutes about the need to embrace risk, strip meaningful assets from competitors, and represent Colts fans who deserved a superior product. This was one of those moments when the words came so easily, I could sort of watch myself talk. I was pointing at the table for added emphasis, and looked Smulyan in the eye throughout my entire presentation.

As I was out of body briefly, I audited the rest of the table. Everyone listened intently, and I was quite proud in the moment of my unique performance. Out of the corner of my eye, I noticed something red at the end of the table. It was odd that I had not noticed it previously, and I refused to look away from Smulyan to check what it was — maybe a red lampshade. When I finished, Jeff smiled and thanked me, and the glowing red ball moved slightly. I looked at it. It was Severino's face.

Tom's head looked like it was going to explode right off his neck.

I knew I screwed up. Badly. But I also was certain that I was right. Young and dumb always values being correct over all else.

Without taking you too deep into the weeds, let me briefly explain what I have learned since that day in 1994 that could have derailed my career. Radio stations that chase play-by-play deals into deep financial risk put every employee at risk. Salespeople chase the cash necessary to offset the payment of the play-by-play contract at the expense of deals that can be done to build business used to cover other operating expenses — usually employee salaries. They take their eyes off what sustains the station in order to pay the contract. The extra $100K that I so blithely dismissed as chump change might cost a bunch of people inside and outside that conference room their jobs.

Severino wasn't mad that I disagreed. He was mad that I did it well enough that jobs — including his — might be lost because I decided my opinion mattered more than the circumspect strategy Severino had employed.

Five years later, Severino and I had dinner with a network rep named Mary, and we shared stories of times we made fools of ourselves in meetings. I had never mentioned that research meeting during subsequent conversations with Severino, and thought this might be a great time to break that ice in a relaxed setting over drinks. "Not sure whether Tom will remember this, but..." I began. Mary laughed and gasped in all the right places.

At the end, I turned to Severino, "Do you remember that, Tom?" He squinted in a barely noticeable way, paused, and without any hint of a smile said, "Yes." Tom Severino forgave a lot, but he never forgot.

By the way, WIBC got the Colts rights, no one lost his or her job as a result of digging $100K deeper, and the station thrived under Severino's leadership until he passed away in 2009. His leadership and friendship are cornerstones of my business and personal philosophies, and I am thrilled to have had him as my friend.

Lessons learned:

1. Make sure you understand the ramifications of your answer before offering it in a meeting with the CEO.

2. Never revisit unpleasant professional moments with the person you made unpleasant — especially when he's your boss.

3. Understand your position in a conference room — even if the CEO doesn't — and behave accordingly.

Desperate and Dateless

No, this chapter is not about my tireless search for an emotional connection with a woman while in college. It's the story of a radio show I hosted that went horribly wrong after a strangely satisfying 13-week run on WIBC in Indianapolis.

The idea for the show was born at the Emmis Communications holiday party in 1994. Some dope thought karaoke would be a lot of fun as a party sideshow while employees ate and drank as much as they could on the company dime. As usual, I decided to sing. I sing not because I enjoy performing, or believe myself to be entertaining to others, but because I tend to loathe the performances of everyone else. My song is both a three-minute break from pretending to be entertained by the warbling of other untalented but well-meaning hacks, and a passive-aggressive act of vengeance toward those I have listened to.

My go-to song is the Charlie Rich classic *The Most Beautiful Girl (in the World)*. It's a simple little song that I can take way over the top, which I find amusing. This was the first — and only — Emmis holiday party attended by my boss, program director Bobby Hatfield, and Bobby liked the way I performed. After I finished, he told me, "Kent, you were meant to be a host. You're a performer. We need to get you

169

a show." Believing his praise was rum-fueled blather, I responded with a shrug and forgot about it.

Five months later, Bobby revisited the idea of making me a radio host. He insisted that even if I wasn't very good at it I would develop some empathy for talent by hosting. They would be more likely to listen to my guidance if they knew I had gone through some of what they experience on a daily basis. At that point I had no designs on being a full-time host, but liked the idea of getting a feel for the challenges of sitting behind a microphone. So I agreed, without asking for any compensation for the effort.

Bobby decided my show would air Saturday nights from 9 p.m. to midnight, and it would be called *Desperate and Dateless*. The conceit of the show was tried and true — a radio classic. I would take calls from people looking for love and try to set them up with other callers who responded to their message. I argued that WIBC's demographic and the show's focus operated in different galaxies. Listeners to WIBC on Saturday nights tended to be old — exceptionally old. "People about to draw their last breath are unlikely to waste it trying to hook up with other nearly-dead listeners," I told Bobby. He called me a synonym for female genitalia, and told me the show would premiere the first Saturday in May.

It's funny what hosts feel as they host a show. During the first episode of *Desperate and Dateless*, I felt the audience was exceptionally confused as I asked them to participate in what amounted to a solicitation for on-air personal ads. Callers confirmed my feeling as they expressed puzzlement and dismay over the show's format. I decided to abandon ship on the format and tell stories. Just prior to the show, I saw a well-known local professional athlete buy a carton of Trojan Magnum condoms at the drug store across the street from the station, and then a giant bag of plums at the Kroger.

I joked that I was immediately embarking on a diet of plums and nothing but plums.

I told stories, and Matt Hibbeln, my board-operator, laughed. He was a good listener, and I appreciated his interest because talking to yourself alone in a room for three hours is a lot more difficult than it sounds. I later hired Matt as Dave "the King" Wilson's producer because of his ability to listen and laugh. He's still at Emmis as WIBC's assistant program director.

The show continued for several weeks, and I was afraid that eventually I would run out of stories, and would need to find actual lonely hearts willing to debase themselves on the radio for the amusement of octagenarians.

We got a break in the middle of June as we had a remote as part of Kroger Circlefest on Monument Circle. I had a stack of concert tickets to give away to drunks who had been worn out by that night's concerts featuring Eddie Money, Rick Springfield, and a knockoff of Creedence Clearwater Revival. There was a crowd of 50 in front of my little stage, and I offered a pair of Sheryl Crow tickets to the person who brought back the most signage from competing radio stations. Every company in town was doing a remote to promote Circlefest, so there was signage everywhere. I staged races around the fountain in the center of Monument Circle where people would run in opposite directions. I also offered tickets to anyone willing to jump into the fountain and splash around. That lasted until the police told me anyone who took a quick dip would be arrested.

One guy came back with an armful of X-103 and Q95 signage. It was not my intent to have a liquored up rube strip clean the Clear Channel area, but I paid off. A guy and a girl raced each other, and the guy won. I gave both one ticket because the girl took a header after her first step and her house dress flipped over her head exposing her undergarments. Oddly, the two who did not know each other before that race attended the concert as a couple and wound up marrying (they were the only couple I successfully paired during the 13-show run).

That show was exhausting, but fun. At the very least I had something to talk about other than begging the elderly to put down their Sudokus and call WIBC.

A few more weeks passed with wasted attempts at prompting calls from singles before I finally snapped. On the last Saturday of July I had a pair of tickets to the Brickyard 400 NASCAR race for the following weekend to give away. I decided to give them to the person who broke up with a significant other in the most hilarious way. This seemed like a great idea at the time, and it provided an evening of unforgettable heartbreak for all of Indianapolis to hear.

The Brickyard was a tough ticket in 1995, and we had callers throughout the show thrilled to have girlfriends pick up a phone so they could dump them. One guy called from the couple's bedroom and said it was time to tell his live-in girlfriend to pack. He kind of whispered into the phone because she was in the next room watching TV. I told him to have her pick up the living room extension. After telling her that she was on the radio, I told the guy he was up. He matter of factly laid it out, "I'd just rather have a pair of tickets to the Brickyard 400 than you as my girlfriend." She started to cry. He held firm. I felt nauseous.

Another guy called from his car and said he was driving to his girlfriend's house to end it in exchange for the tickets. We kept him on until he arrived, knocked on the door, and then told the poor woman they were through. She cried, and he laughed.

When we spontaneously launched this contest, I thought we would have as many takers for the break-ups as we had the previous 11 weeks for hook-ups — zero — but the break-up show was not not only more popular, it was better radio in a truly hideous way. I couldn't stop listening, which was good because it was my job.

True to our word, we gave away the tickets to the guy who called from the bedroom because we had the woman on the phone and got to hear her reaction with better fidelity than the woman at the door.

That night I decided hosting a radio show that eagerly engaged the worst instincts of greed in our listeners was not for me. No more break-ups, and no more raunchy giveaways. I would only put people together, even if it meant talking to myself for three hours.

The next week was the final *Desperate and Dateless*. The show was to immediately follow Donald Davidson's *Talk of Gasoline Alley*, which was to follow the Brickyard 400. Donald loves the history of the Indianapolis Motor Speedway, and lovers of that history love Donald. They call with arcane questions about open wheel racing, and Donald enjoys providing otherwise unavailable factoids about the Indy 500. Normally, this is a fun show. Not that day.

Rain was forecast on that first Saturday in August of 1995, and it did rain for awhile. Then the rain stopped, but not likely in time to dry the track well enough for the cars to run safely for all 160 laps before dark . A member of the WIBC staff reported the race would not be run that day — it would be pushed to Sunday — according to a NASCAR official. As a result, thousands of fans packed their coolers, left the bleachers, and headed for home.

At 3:40 that afternoon, NASCAR ordered drivers to their cars, and by 4:05 the green flag flew. Needless to say, fans who trusted what they heard on WIBC were livid. That anger spilled onto the air during Donald's show, and Donald didn't

quite know how to handle the vitriol. Donald is a well —
mannered and friendly Englishman who fell in love with
the Indianapolis Motor Speedway as a young man in
London. His comfort zone as a broadcaster does not extend
to calming incensed race fans.

After 20 minutes of listening to an exasperated Donald
discourage those angry with WIBC from calling the station,
I decided to relieve him. Over my two years at WIBC, I had
fielded hundreds of complaint calls and had become pretty
good at talking to furious listeners.

I started at 8:30 p.m., and was quickly joined by Bobby
(the program director who insisted I host *Desperate and
Dateless*), who walked into the studio with a 12-pack of
Budweiser. As I apologized to the next caller, Bobby decided
he had taken all the crap he needed to. He got after a caller
pretty good, and I can't remember who called who "a turd,"
but I went to break and told Bobby to go home. I don't know
much about calculus, but I did know Beer + Bobby + angry
listeners = great radio likely to cost WIBC its license.

I told listeners to call and vent, and promised every single
call would be taken. I tried to exhaust the anger that night
so it wouldn't fester and result in a Monday of misery. One
way or another, those angry fans were going to wind up
calling me anyway, so why not get it over with during a
period when I would normally be begging them to hook up
with one another? And my groveling was better radio than
the typical show anyway. The calls finally ended at 1:10 a.m.

The next Wednesday, Bobby's tenure with WIBC came
to an abrupt end, and with it came an equally abrupt end to
our little Saturday night experiment. After Bobby left, general
manager Tom Severino asked what I would do first as a
program director. I said, "Cancel *Desperate and Dateless*." Tom
smiled and nodded.

Thirteen shows, 39 hours, 156 segments, some laughs, some humiliations, a great producer/board-op hired, and one happy couple united because an over-served Hoosier flopped out of the gate at the outset of an ill-advised footrace.

Lessons learned:

1. Never sing karaoke.

2. Never work for free.

3. When the shit you are fed by listeners/customers is justified, grab a spoon.

4. Never announce cancellation or postponement of an event until the event is actually cancelled or postponed.

Making Youth Baseball Fun Again

All parents enjoy hearing praise about their child, so when people first invite them to play travel (insert sport here), the parent is likely to say yes before vetting the opportunity. I sure did.

When Ryan was nine, he was a pretty good left-handed pitcher, and I was his coach. Our team was loaded with talented athletes — three of our 12 players played varsity baseball (one of whom was a two-year starter at quarterback), one nearly won a state title in the 100 and 200 yard dashes, and Ryan played basketball in college. A reasonably competitive coach would have gone undefeated. We finished with a 7-7 record.

My dad was my coach when I was nine, and he was a damn smart baseball coach and fan. Our team finished 1-8-1 — not because we lacked talent, but because his top priority was the enjoyment of the game. Our youth baseball games were about playing, laughing, and popsicles. Dad kept the mood light, and everyone had a great time.

I was convinced Dad had it right, so the team I coached that season was all about learning how to play the game by making mistakes. There was no judgment — only light — hearted instruction. Kids were shifted all over the field, and they hit in a variety of spots in the batting order. My only limitations were to make sure we put kids in a position where they could succeed. Pitchers had to demonstrate an ability to throw strikes, and catchers had to be able to, well, catch- and return the ball accurately to the pitcher.

At the first practice, I asked who wanted to pitch. My son and an athletic kid named Taylor said they did, and three others came too. Taylor threw first, and I told him to hit the mitt. His arms and legs went every which way and the ball went three feet over my head. I talked to him for a minute about simplifying his motion and thinking about hitting the mitt instead of throwing hard. His next five pitches hit the pocket of my mitt right where I held it. I was sure for about a half-minute that I might have been the finest pitching coach in the history of the game.

The next three kids proved my self-aggrandizing theory false. Baseballs flew everywhere. It turned out that Taylor was just a hell of an athlete and great kid.

One of those three kids who wanted to pitch had a dad who insisted he should pitch. I worked with the kid in practice. He could throw hard, but his control was nonexistent. I tried to explain to the dad that if I sent him out and he walked everyone he faced, it could haunt him forever. So, until he showed the ability to throw strikes, he would play elsewhere.

I went through something similar when I was a kid.

When I was eight years-old, I took tennis lessons for the first time (tennis was huge when I was a kid). My best friend was a kid named Tom whose dad was a collegiate tennis coach, so we played doubles against some other kids after one of the lessons. I double-faulted an entire game, and felt embarrassed. Tom was fine about it until we got back to his family's house. His mom asked how Tom played. Tom replied, "It was great, except for Kent double-faulting a whole game. I mean, have you ever even heard of that? An entire game!" My second serve sucked forever after that. What has happened to Charles Barkley's golf swing happened to my second serve. I never even swung the racquet. I just kind of swatted at the ball.

I wasn't going to put a kid in the position to be defined forever in his mind and those of his teammates by a developmental and temporary inability to throw strikes. It just seemed cruel, so he didn't pitch that year. As a high school player, he became a very good pitcher, so I was pleased for both he and his dad.

Other coaches ran the gamut from very cool with the kids to psychotic screamers. There was one coach who even ran behind the plate, climbed the backstop, and screamed at our pitcher. To the kid's credit, he focused through it and threw strikes. It occurred to me briefly that I should respond by pulling the coach off the backstop and beat his ass, but that seemed like the kind of thing that would send a terrible message to a bunch of nine-year-olds, even if it made me feel great for a few seconds.

Tryouts for the travel team were conducted, and I had two kids selected for the A team. My son was one of them. I was asked to be an assistant coach, which was kind of nice. At least I would get more quality time with Ryan, and if the head coach turned out to be a lunatic, I could help mitigate the harm he could do. Little did I know.

The coach was worse than a lunatic — he was a humorless lunatic. Practices were tedious, and games were bizarre meditations about the many ways baseball could be crushingly miserable for a bunch of third and fourth graders. After one especially dispirited performance, the coach asked the assistant coaches to stay in the dugout while he walked the team toward deep centerfield for a meeting. I assumed he wanted to clear the decks of adults so he could apologize for turning what should be fun into monotonous drudgery.

The team walked back no happier than when they walked out. I asked Ryan what the coach said. Ryan answered, "Oh, he yelled at us some more."

The next practice was completely devoid of energy and spirit. The shortstop and third baseman weren't charging ground balls as player after player took their cuts in what had become the routine batting practice marathon. I took a position behind them and started hustling a little bit to beat them to ground balls. They started charging, and all of a sudden the three of us were smiling and having a great time playing baseball.

Five minutes after we began getting after it, the coach stopped pitching and asked what we were doing. I said, "We're having fun charging ground balls!"

He told us to stop that. The third baseman, who was the son of the coach hung his head. "Sorry," he said quietly.

I had three options. I could leave the team and my son in the hands of this buffoon who had yet to grasp nine-year-olds are supposed to have fun playing baseball. I don't quit, so that was out — plus, the closer I was to Ryan, the better I could manage his happiness. Or, I could leave and take Ryan with me. That had some plusses and minuses. A plus was to show Ryan that some authority figures are boobs and don't deserve your respect or attention. The minus was to set an example of quitting when things became unpleasant. I elected option three — gut it out until the end of the summer because the hard road sometimes brings unexpected rewards.

There could have been a fourth option — confronting the coach with some kind of behavioral intervention, but I've learned over the years that well-meaning morons are poor learners. A positive result seemed unlikely in the extreme, and the season was only a couple of weekends from ending. No kid should be forced to look forward to the end of baseball season, but maybe out of this debacle something good might come.

And it did.

A couple of months into the offseason, I got a phone call from one of the parents from the team of misery. A group of renegades had decided to throw in and create a travel team outside the purview of the organization that ran youth baseball in Fishers, Indiana. The dads met, commiserated, drank many beers, put together a list of attributes needed for success, and committed to doing it differently. The coach would be a highly organized Indianapolis firefighter, who had a practice plan timed to the second.

The team, the Fishers Marlins, was comprised of good players with supportive parents. Most importantly, the moms and dads knew and liked each other. At the very least, the parents were going to have a hell of a good time, which is more important than you might think. Miserable parents tend to be contagious, and we had been down that road the previous summer.

One of our first games was against the Carmel Dad's Club. (Nothing against Carmel, but who the hell names their team after a bunch of dads? How self-immersed were these people?) Our first mission was to eliminate all negative chatter that might evoke the mood of the previous summer. All plays were praised — even mistakes. A kid named Adam hit a line drive outside the right field line, and the coaches cheered it like a home run. My mom and dad were at the game, and Dad yelled at me while I coached first base, "What the hell is the matter with you? What is this, the love team?"

Damn right it was. One unpleasant summer was plenty.

There was a game in Greenfield the next weekend against a good team with an eccentric coach who wore a full uniform right down to the spikes. Here was this 40-ish guy in the same garb as a bunch of 10-year-olds. It was not only strange — it was wrong. As has been the case most of my life, I find more joy in doing the opposite of those I don't respect than imitating those I do. I immediately went to Target and bought Hawaiian shirts for all the coaches. We wore them as our uniform every game thereafter.

We did everything we could to make baseball fun — like it should be for children.

One interesting outgrowth of our three summers of love playing and coaching baseball was realizing competitive kids relentlessly push themselves, and would break down emotionally after failure. We tried to tell them how baseball — and life — is about what's coming next and not what's been, and that tears are a reflection of disappointment for what's been. None of our well-intentioned chatter mattered. The kids were just wound a little tight, and hated what they perceived to be failure.

Ten years later, almost all of the 12 Marlins played collegiate sports. Ryan played basketball at Loyola. Kyle played golf at Butler. Justin ran cross country and track at Butler. Matt played baseball at Purdue. Max played football at John Carroll and the University of Indianapolis. Taylor played baseball at DePauw. All of the kids played a variety of sports in high school.

For those next three summers, the Marlins competed, laughed, cried, and shared the game of baseball with each other. The parents also laughed, grew to be friends, and hosted team parties that were as much for us as the kids. How many games and tournaments did the Marlins win? I have no idea, and I would be disappointed if I did. This team was about love and fun, not winning, and that's as it should be in youth sports.

Lessons learned:

1. Build youth sports teams around a group of parents who enjoy each other. You might not win a bunch of games, but you're going to have a great time.

2. Coaches should invite input from everyone, so all feel an investment in the result. Pretty good lesson for business owners and managers, too.

3. Winning is not a goal — it's a result.

4. Out of misery, beauty can grow.

5. Youth sports coaches should embrace the notion that they are not coaching players, but future players who will coach their kids.

6. Tightly-wound kids can't be loosened — and they shouldn't be.

Don't Mess
with Riptides

On our last day of a spring break vacation in Orange Beach, Alabama, my 14-year-old son and I ran into the Gulf of Mexico to body surf. The waves were an impressive six feet, and it looked like we were about to have as much fun as we deserved on this last morning before we hopped in the car for our 10-hour drive back to Indianapolis.

My wife yelled after us, "Hey, look at the flags!" I waved her off. Red flags were everywhere, but the waves were manageable.

By the way, I am not a water guy. Going in the ocean defies all reason. There are jellyfish, sharks, eels, rays, and all kinds of other aquatic stuff that can cause harm for land bound mammals like us.

I am exactly as uncomfortable in the water as fish are on land, but this was vacation and our condo was on the beach, so I indulged in some creative mind-screwing that would allow me to enjoy the thrill of catching a great wave and being hurled toward the beach.

The day before we left for vacation, I slathered some goop on my scalp for a couple of hours and when I rinsed my hair it was yellow. Whenever I saw my reflection, I laughed and remembered that this was a time to shun responsibilities and enjoy life. When we returned to Indianapolis, I would get out the clippers and shear the yellow mop so I wouldn't look insane when I returned to work.

Ryan and I waded out to where the water was waist deep, but the waves were breaking a little farther out, so I went chest deep. Ryan had a slightly concerned look on his face as though he could sense danger. I shrugged it off, "Not coming out?" Ryan shook his head no.

The first wave was perfect, and I flew down its face and then tumbled. The second was even better, but when I looked toward the beach it seemed I was about 20 yards beyond where I started. Ryan looked at me and then Julie, and for the first time I was a little concerned.

I rode another wave, and now I was far enough out that I couldn't touch bottom with my head above water. *Riptide* is a word at which I had always scoffed. Fools and idiots get caught in riptides. Every time I heard of someone drowning as the result of a riptide, I said the same thing — "What a moron!" I had entered a realm of recreational water fun that potentially cast me as the next moron.

A riptide is a relatively strong, narrow current flowing outward from the beach through the surf zone that presents a hazard to swimmers. They are most often caused by a breech in a sand bar where water rushes out to sea. Whatever it was, I had to figure out how to get the hell out of it.

The waves were mostly rhythmic, so I could bob up, get a lungful of air, and then submerge. Because of the size of the waves, treading water was impossible. I looked to the beach again, which seemed to be roughly 100 yards away. Ryan looked at Julie with his palms up as though he wanted her input on whether he should head out on an ill-advised rescue mission. Thank God Julie shook her head no.

I continued bobbing up and down and remained calm. I thought, *This cannot be how I go — Ryan and Julie waiting by the shore for the ocean to return my yellow-haired corpse to them. Then they have to crate me and send me back to Indy. I have to rescue myself right now because this is the level of idiocy that defines people and their families forever. Julie, Ryan and my mom crying over me looking like this? Friends, family, even strangers would say 'Oh yeah, Sterling — the bleach-blond dumbass who got caught in a riptide and croaked. What a moron!'*

The lesson I have always heard is that riptides are narrow, so if you swim parallel to the beach 20 yards or so, the current returns to normal and you can easily get back to safe harbor. At this point I was getting really tired, so I had to make the call to use whatever strength I had left to move sideways or just try to bonsai it to Ryan and Julie.

Finally, I thought, *Screw swimming parallel. If I only have one shot, I'm not drowning because I swam toward more water.* I came to the top one more time, managed a big gulp of air, and swam as hard as I could toward the beach.

By no means would I ever be described as a strong swimmer, but on that day a switch must have flipped, or the current suddenly changed. I swam as frantically as I could, and actually felt great in the water. I moved swiftly toward the beach, and within a couple of minutes I was standing next to Ryan. But I could barely stand.

Ryan helped me to the beach. It's funny how after being buoyant and strong in the water, I felt like I weighed a half ton. Julie looked at me with pity and a little horror. She asked if I was okay. I told her I was tired. She said, "You look gray."

Of all the colors a body can be, I think gray is one of the worst — not as bad as green or purple, but really bad. Dead people look gray. I might have been gray, but I wasn't dead. My son and wife didn't have to fish me out of the sea.

Looking back, this episode is not among my favorites. I failed to respect water, and it almost killed me. Worse, it almost caused my lasting image to be that of an idiot who caused his family unnecessary pain, and crafted a legacy as a dolt. But it also provided a moment of clarity while I was under the waves. Thoughts become very clear when a life is in peril. I can still see the waves crashing above me, and recall believing that whatever value my life had in that moment, it was not going to end in the ocean.

That day represented a new start for me. Not to get maudlin, but it brought a better understanding that everyday is a gift to enjoy and invest in.

I have not gone in the ocean since, and I do not plan to. I never enjoyed it in the first place, so I've chosen to embrace my disdain for large bodies of water in which I could drown. But I wouldn't change a thing from that morning in the Gulf of Mexico.

Lessons learned:

1. Don't mess with angry water — *ever*!

2. Look at the flags at the beach — *always*!

3. Do a quick analysis of the upside and downside of every activity. If the potential cost outweighs the potential fun, do not engage!

4. The Taoist principle of water deserving respect is well — founded.

5. Don't bleach your hair or alter your appearance in any way that family would need to explain if you died.

Never Bring a Quick Wit to a Gun Fight

Tensions run high at youth basketball tournaments — especially among spectators during close games between teams that don't care for one another. Parents get in on the act all too often, embarrassing everyone involved — especially the kids. When our son Ryan's team played, my strategy was to videotape every game so I would be distracted from the temptation to shout things at players, referees, or parents.

That worked — most of the time.

One of the more memorable exceptions occurred in Dallas as my son's seventh grade Indy Wolves team played the D-1 Greyhounds. The Greyhounds had two gifted players, O.J. Mayo and Bill Walker. Mayo, who was selected third overall in the 2008 NBA draft, was thought to be the best player in the country in the high school class of 2007, and Walker might have been even more athletic than Mayo.

In the early 2000s, competing with a team that featured a future NBA lottery pick meant the officiating was going to be skewed toward the kid who brought fans into the gym. That was just the reality at that point because that's how organizers made a little extra cash. No tournament wanted a team with Mayo, Eric Gordon, Derrick Rose, Kevin Love or any of the other studs of that class bowing out early, so our game against the Greyhounds was more like five on seven than a fair fight.

Normally, the fans of each team sit on opposite sides of the court, but for some reason fans of the Greyhounds were all over the place. At least we assumed they were fans of the Greyhounds. No one other than family members ever came to our games to cheer for the Wolves, especially in Dallas. Seventh graders other than Mayo didn't draw much of a crowd — to the credit of the fans, who should not be drawn to basketball played by seventh graders.

I kept my mind occupied by videotaping the game while my wife seethed over the refs favoring the Greyhounds. Being a former player herself, Julie is knowledgeable and able to deliver gut-punch critiques of referees. She was on this crew pretty good on that hot Dallas afternoon.

She was so annoying to the fans of the Greyhounds that one gentleman who was identified to me later as Mayo's grandfather (most of the fans in attendance seemed to be related to Mayo one way or another) took loud and profane exception. "Why don't you shut up, fucking bitch!"

Uh-oh!

I can tolerate any level of unpleasantness aimed toward me. Call me a name or insult my intellect, I smile and move on. Come after Julie, and my temperament changes. I moved toward the floor from the fifth row as the whistle blew. One of the two refs was right next to me, so I decided to talk to Mayo's grandfather through the ref. "This guy just called my wife a 'fucking bitch', and either you're going to do something about it, or I'm going to stick my foot in his ass!"

At no point did I make eye contact with the grandfather while I spoke to the ref. My play was to let Julie know I had her back while communicating that fan misbehavior was on the verge of causing a crowd control issue. This was an old guy, and I wasn't going to knock him around because he yelled at Julie — at least not without trying to get referees involved.

Gramps got up immediately and left the gym. I silently congratulated myself for putting an end to the unpleasantness with my strategic indirect dressing down. It was more than a little surprising that he abandoned the game to avoid another tongue lashing, but maybe I was just that imposing.

I have been called many things during my lifetime, but imposing is not among them, so I walked myself back from believing I was my generation's Dirty Harry. Regardless, the threat was no longer imminent, so I went back to videotaping the game.

A few minutes later, Bob Ashworth — a fellow Wolves parent and one of the finest high school football coaches in Indiana history — waved me down to his row. "Hey, I'm not saying the guy who yelled at Julie is carrying a gun, but when he left the gym there was no bulge in his pocket, and now there is one," he said. "And I don't think it's because he's happy to see you."

Well, that was a different kettle of fish. In a war of words, I'm relatively agile and skilled. In a fistfight, the worst that can happen is a broken nose. With guns, I'm unarmed — always. At the moment of the grandfather's liking, he could stand, point, and shoot.

For the rest of the game I kept one eye on the camera and the other eye on gramps. After the game I waited for the kids, as I was the driver of the 12-passenger van transporting the players. After they got safely into the van, I made the walk from the gym to the van just in case Grandpa Mayo was waiting to plug me.

Obviously the old guy didn't shoot, and other than Ashworth giving me a heads-up, I have no reason to suspect he went outside to get a gun. Although I doubt it, he might have gone for a walk because he felt bad about referring to Julie in an overtly profane way. Who knows? The only thing I know for sure about that episode is that pondering the existence of a gun in the pocket of a guy who is far from happy with me prompts a unique level of nervousness. It wasn't fear, but there was a feeling that the situation could change without notice, and that anything could happen. The three of us had climbed to the end of the skinny limb together, and if it snapped we needed to be ready to act.

I went through a series of hypothetical responses to Crazy Grandpa going off the rails, and understood that with every minute that passed, the environment became just a little calmer. The game went on and the officials continued missing calls, which went unchallenged by my wife or anyone else.

The Wolves lost to Mayo and Walker by nine, which probably helped Mayo's elderly relative get over the strange interlude with the couple from Indiana who were willing to match him crazy for crazy.

That night we grilled steak and swam. Later, the parents enjoyed a couple of beers and I grabbed the camcorder to play back the game. In the mayhem of Julie yelling at the refs, Grandpa Mayo yelling at Julie, and me threatening Grandpa Mayo, I forgot to stop recording. There it was, the pristine audio of our near fracas with tilted video of the bleachers. What I quoted earlier is exactly what was said between us.

It was the kind of idiotic video that people might reflexively laugh at on social media today, and I'm glad this happened in 2002 before all of that silliness was invented. The parents watched the video that night, and most laughed.

It was silly and harmless, minus the possible involvement of a gun. It was also angry and idiotic, and didn't have to end harmlessly.

Lessons learned:

1. Take care in whom you threaten with violence. You know you're just talking, but maybe the other guy thinks you're serious.

2. Never back down, but no need to poke twice a bear packing heat.

3. Crazy parents should sit on opposite sides of the gym, and a physical barrier is not the worst idea.

Innocent Hijinx Gone Awry

All I heard was a moan and some gasps from our friends in the pool. There was no other response to what I thought was a fun and lighthearted gesture with a water balloon — no laughs, no admonishments, just hands over mouths and silence. Of all possible responses, silence was the worst.

A group of nine of us, some friends and others just acquaintances, headed south to Delray Beach, Florida, for spring break, and this was Day 1. We stayed in a hotel with a nice pool 50-feet from a bar and a four-iron from the beach. The mood was exuberant and nothing kicks fun up a notch like water balloons. I filled 25 balloons with water, and time came to unleash hell on friends and family.

The first target was my son, who was about to disappear behind a storage shed adjacent to the far side of the pool. I was on the second floor balcony, and launched like a World War II infantryman lobbing a grenade into a Japanese bunker. Cue the moans and gasps. My first toss was a direct hit, catching Ryan right in the man nuggets. Julie rushed to Ryan, who I could not see because of the shed. The odds of a blind shot blasting a 14-year-old right in the pills as he walked upright had to be a million to one for any normal human being, but for me, given my penchant for the worst possible result, it would be about an even money wager.

Julie came out from behind the shed, and was furious. "What the hell is the matter with you? How could you do that to your son?" I was still unsure about exactly what I had done, and had the remnants of a smile on my face. "Whatever you think is happening here, it isn't funny!" she screamed.

I ran down the steps to check on Ryan who was still writhing in pain when I reached the scene. The water balloon, unbroken, rested next to Ryan, and he was clearly agitated that roughly a half pint of latex-encased liquid had fallen from the sky unannounced slamming into his most sensitive area.

I waited as he got to his feet and regained his composure. He was angry for a brief moment, and then jumped in the pool where the cool water served as a pain and swelling suppressant. When I sheepishly joined the group, they looked at me like I had committed a war crime. I shrugged. "Innocent hijinx gone awry." That was my effort to explain what happened, and it became our rallying cry for the week.

Ryan and I had been down this road before. Before his first year of youth baseball as a nine-year-old, I asked if he wanted to put on the gear and try to learn to be a catcher. He's left-handed, so catching was out as a serious vocation, but it's always good to try something new so, he threw on the shin guards, chest protector, and mask, and we walked to the field across the street.

I had read former Cubs catcher Randy Hundley's account of how he taught his son Todd (also a former Cubs catcher) to catch, and I thought the protocol he described sounded pretty good. First thing Randy did with Todd was throw pitches in the dirt to test his son's toughness. Ryan was padded up from the top of his head to the top of his feet, and I couldn't throw harder than 70 miles an hour, so what could go wrong? I reared back and fired a one-hopper straight into Ryan's testicles. In my enthusiasm to engage in a baseball activity as a coach with my son for the first time, I had completely forgotten the most vital protective device any man can wear — a cup.

For those who are unfamiliar with a cup, it's a hard plastic shell cushioned on the edges that can be inserted into a jockstrap to protect a man's nether region. I hated wearing one, and usually didn't. It never occurred to me to provide Ryan with a cup, so when that first one-hopper bounced past his glove and into the place where his legs come together, he crumpled to the ground in a groaning heap.

When I helped Ryan through the front door, Julie reacted as good mothers do — with extreme concern. Then Ryan and I explained what happened, and concern became anger. "Are you an idiot?" she asked. When I tried to respond, Julie informed me her question was rhetorical. I apologized to Ryan, and we shelved any thought of his becoming a catcher. He would be a pitcher and first baseman, where his groin was less likely to be concussed.

One last peculiar piece of parenting that caused Ryan some physical trauma occurred at a postseason party after his first year of summer basketball. The season had gone ridiculously well for this group of soon-to-be fifth graders. They finished second in nationals, and for a neighborhood team, that was a hell of an accomplishment. The team got along exceptionally well, and that included the parents.

The party was held at a country club with a pool, and the kids did not waste their opportunity to swim. Because some 10-year-olds enjoy physical challenges, they attacked the high dive. They performed flips, twists, and all kinds of challenging dives. Ryan stood on the sidelines and enjoyed the exploits of the other guys. I thought it would be fun for Ryan to get out of his comfort zone and do something creative, so I walked up to him and said, "Do something."

He was puzzled. "Do something fun off the high dive — you know — like your teammates."

Ryan recoiled a little bit, and I reaffirmed my belief that life is more fun for those who do things rather than watch things. He dutifully climbed the ladder, looked at me, and then the water. He walked to the edge of the board, jumped, and bounded skyward. From that point forward, Ryan's descent was a nightmare for everyone.watching, and it played out in slow motion. Instead of spinning or turning, Ryan's body stayed in the same horizontal position when his jump reached its apex. As he plummeted toward the water, the group who had encouraged the kids with their cheers went silent. Just before Ryan and the water met, he somehow managed to lower both his head and feet so the impact was very much like a cupped hand slapping the surface — except this was an entire body.

The sound of the impact was different from anything I have ever heard. It was a very loud "Thwap!" People reflexively ran away from pool side, and there was a chorus of "OOOOOOOO" from everyone at the pool. This wasn't a belly flop. It was much more violent, like a body landing on cement. The impact was so violent, I'm not sure Ryan's back ever got wet. He just kind of laid on top of the water after landing, rather than sinking.

He gingerly moved toward the edge of the pool, and made a quiet noise of anguish with whatever air remained in his lungs. I apologized, and Ryan said, "Why did you make me do that?" I tried to explain that what happened was not exactly what I had in mind without giving him the sense that I blamed him for not executing a double flip with a twist. Ryan had always been able to get his body to do what he visualized, so it never occurred to me that he would fall flat onto — not into — the water.

On the plus side, everyone in the pool area visited Ryan to express their concern and admiration for his singularly horrific flop.

Not all goof-ups between Ryan and I were water-related.

When Ryan was two-years-old, Julie worked at Illinois Masonic Hospital, and if I wasn't working that day we would pop over for a little visit. The hospital was three blocks from our apartment, so it was an easy walk and made the day a little shorter for Julie.

We took the elevator to Julie's office on the third floor,. We had been there before, so Ryan and I walked without holding hands as we got off the elevator. But Ryan suddenly hung an abrupt u-turn and jumped back on the empty elevator as its doors closed.

Ryan was gone to wherever that elevator was headed next. I weighed the pros and cons of chasing the elevator, but thought it was best to stay right there. I hit both the up and down buttons for the bank of three elevators and hoped Ryan was still on it the next time his elevator returned. If that elevator door opened and Ryan wasn't on it, I would have to call security and ask that they lock down the building until we found the little adventurer.

It's funny how a day can go from normal, happy, and routine to hysterical in the time it takes for an elevator door to close. What if the elevator went to the sixth floor? That's where the psych ward was. Yikes! All kinds of potential disasters careened through my brain as I kept hitting buttons to get that elevator door to open — hopefully with my two-year-old boy on it.

Just as I had hoped, the elevator returned with a smiling little boy ready to visit his mom. Adventuresome enough to hop on an elevator, but smart enough to stay on it. That defines Ryan just as well at age 31 as at two.

Ryan and I were separated one more time 16 years later. After he graduated high school, one of his gifts was a two-day trip to New York for a Mets night game at the soon-to-close Shea Stadium, followed by an afternoon contest between the Yankees and Twins at the soon-to-close Yankee Stadium. We flew into LaGuardia and cabbed to our hotel in Flushing. We had several hours until the Mets game, so we decided to hop on the Seven train to Manhattan to explore Times Square, the Empire State Building, and other landmarks.

The stop where we boarded was at the end of the line, so we hopped on a subway car as it sat and waited to go. A train rolled up on the other track, and quickly left. I surmised we were on the wrong train, and when another train came to a stop on the other track, I said, "Let's go!" I hopped off, and before Ryan could follow me, the doors closed on our original train and it rolled out with Ryan on it. He meekly waved as I stood alone on the platform.

This was in 2007, and cell coverage was not good underground. Calling or texting Ryan was impossible, and my mind raced to all the bad outcomes of this typical Sterling course of events. What if Ryan's phone ran out of battery or he accidentally dropped it down a sewer? What if he got off and tried to double back as I was on a train moving toward him?

The next train left a few minutes later, and once it moved above ground I called Ryan to direct him to meet at his next stop. It all worked out and we had a great time watching baseball at two historic stadiums on their last legs. The best baseball moment was one even a Cubs fan could relish at Yankee Stadium — Mariano Rivera being summoned from the bullpen to Metallica's "Enter Sandman" to lock down a save.

Rivera's performance was drama-free as usual, unlike many of our other adventures.

Lessons learned:

1. Don't throw things at your child — even fun things like water balloons.

2. Mandate catchers wear a cup — even if they don't know what a cup is.

3. Enter and exit trains and elevators with your children, and hold their hands — until they turn 30.

4. Let your child do what he or she is comfortable doing. Sometimes kids stay in their comfort zone for a very good reason.

Flowers for MyStar —
Or Pranks Burn Bridges

Ratings are a silly measurement of radio success, but they are taken very seriously by those who manage or sell the medium. Without getting bogged down in the minutiae of radio ratings, they fluctuate without reason or explanation. When ratings where you work go up, there is an understanding that what goes up usually goes down, but you celebrate anyway. When they go down, you complain about ratings being unfair or how the news/sports/music cycle didn't favor your format.

One afternoon, Tom, Jon, and I were celebrating a particularly good ratings report and noticed a decline across a competitor's three stations. Tom was the general manager, and he and I were riffing on what we might do to have a little fun at our competitor's failures. "We should send MyStar (the name of the company that owned the three stations) a funereal flower arrangement with a card that reads 'So sorry for your loss!'" I said. Everyone laughed.

Tom decided that was perfect, and offered to pay for it. Jon was our program director, and he didn't like the idea at all, "This is not a good idea. You should not do this, and I want no part of it." When in doubt, I side with the guy laughing the loudest. That was Tom.

When I got home, I called a local flower shop and placed the order. The woman on the phone asked for my credit card, and I insisted upon paying in cash. She said it would have to wait until the next day if I wanted to bring in cash because they were closing in five minutes. I explained that I was only 10 minutes away, and could get there if they were willing to stick around a few minutes after closing. She declined.

There are moments in life where a divine providence reaches down from the heavens to help a wayward soul who is about to make a cataclysmic error, and this was one of those times. Interpreting that moment correctly was beyond my meager capabilities. All I knew was that I was going to put into motion some harmless fun, and a store closing would not short-circuit it.

I agreed to provide my credit card number, but demanded the woman swear my name would never be revealed. She took the oath, which I realized then — as you do now — was a useless non-binding gesture. She asked what I would like the card to say. "So sorry for your loss," I said, exactly what Tom and I discussed at our little laughfest. Then I added what I thought was a stroke of genius, "from your friends at Susquehanna."

Susquehanna was the owner of another competing radio station group in Indianapolis, and involving them as a third party would raise the ante and increase the confusion. Genius!

I went to bed confident that laughs were in our immediate future as the managers of MyStar and Susquehanna squared off. What happened in reality was just a little different.

The flowers arrived in the MyStar general manager's office the following morning while he was coincidentally on the phone with the general manager at Susquehanna. According to people privy to the conversation, it went something like this:

"What the hell are these flowers for? Sorry for your loss? Oh, that's very funny!"

"I don't know what you're talking about."

"The funereal arrangement!"

"What funereal arrangement?"

"The one you sent. I'm looking at the card, and it's signed, 'From your friends at Susquehanna!'"

"I didn't send you a funereal arrangement. Who's the florist?"

The MyStar general manager shared the name of the florist.

The manager from Susquehanna told the MyStar manager the florist was a longtime client of his stations. He then called the florist and asked who sent the flowers to MyStar. And of course, because I paid with a credit card and oaths don't mean a damn thing compared to a relationship between a client and radio company, my name was shared.

I was called into Christine's office early the next day. Christine was Tom's boss, and in almost 10 years I had never been called by Christine for anything. She is an unfailingly nice woman — always cordial and friendly. When I walked in, she asked that I close the door. That's never a good sign.

"Okay, here's the thing," she said. "You sent flowers to MyStar, right?" I told her I had. "Normally, that would be funny, but in this case, it isn't because Jeff (our owner) and Mickey (MyStar's owner) had just declared a kind of truce after years of not getting along. Mickey found out you sent the flowers, and now the relationship has cooled again. This is not a good thing. I know it was just a prank, but sometimes these things have repercussions we cannot control."

That was it. I sat there waiting for something else, like "Today is your last day here." It didn't come. Christine thanked me, and sent me back to my office.

I went straight to Tom's office. "Hey, you know, the flower thing blew up. I guess it got to the Jeff and Mickey level, and there are problems."

Tom said he knew, and was about to go up to Chris's office to explain his role in our juvenile joke. That was a hell of a gesture for a GM. Sharing the blame for a juvenile little joke was above and beyond for a guy with kids in college. Most would have limited liability to the dumbass too enthusiastic and stupid to avoid attaching his name to the event via a credit card.

Sadly, that was not nearly the end of the butterfly effect of this little joke. Several years later, lung cancer took Tom. Three months after that, the boss from Susquehanna was hired as his replacement. Four months later, I became the former program director at WIBC and 1070 the Fan.

I'm not saying I was fired because of a stupid little joke from five years prior, but it certainly did not help my brand value with the manager. It's likely I would have been punted regardless because I had worked for Tom for 15 years and was seen as a "Tom guy," which I proudly remain.

The manager brought in his own managers, and that was that.

There are four lessons in this chapter, and I really hope you embrace one of them, although I won't tell you which.

Lessons learned:

1. Pranks are for children. Adults who try to embarrass other adults by playing practical jokes are childish, ridiculous, and generally a lot of fun to be around.

2. Want to know an area that doesn't exist on a resume'? The "Why are you fun to be around?" section.

3. Pranks are like mini-crimes. Extreme care should be taken to minimize evidence that leads victims back to the author.

4. Never cut funny, and that dopey prank remains funny 15 years later.

Dream Comes True by Firing a Great Guy

Working as the assistant program director at WIBC for 13 years wasn't easy. I knew I was capable of being the program director, as did program director Jon Quick. He often recommended I make myself available for that position at talk radio stations around the country. But my family enjoyed living in Indianapolis and my wife and I didn't want to schlep our son all over the country as I chased radio gigs, so I never sought out another position.

Instead, I prepared to be the program director and eagerly accepted any leadership responsibility that would enhance my position to be the obvious choice if Jon ever decided to leave the station. He and market manager Tom Severino were close, so it never occurred to me that a change might be made that would elevate me at Jon's expense.

Emmis Communications owned several radio stations in Indianapolis, including WIBC, one of the leading news/talk stations in the country. WIBC was the city's station of record and regularly won Marconi and Crystal Awards for excellence, but its position on the AM dial was becoming a limitation. Older listeners still found the station, but people in their 20s just didn't listen to AM radio in Indianapolis, so there were discussions about moving WIBC to the FM dial.

I was a huge proponent of WIBC sliding to FM for a variety of reasons — the most important being that it was the right thing to do for the station, its employees, and the community. WIBC was an important conduit of information and insight for central Indiana, and I felt its sustainability relied upon reaching the widest possible audience. A move to FM would facilitate that. My selfish hope was that the AM position WIBC abandoned in favor of the FM band would be filled by a sportstalk product that I would be selected to program.

After a series of meetings, that's exactly what happened, and for 18-months I was blissfully challenged by the process of building 1070 the Fan as Indy's sports voice. We hired Indianapolis Star award-winning columnist Bob Kravitz and sports public relations icon Eddie White to host afternoon drive, and added former Indiana University basketball coach Dan Dakich to host middays. The station was rolling, and I was finally able to enjoy running the programming for a radio station.

Roughly a year after we launched 1070 the Fan, our market manager became ill — really ill. Severino was bothered by back issues, and a scan showed lung cancer had weakened his bones. His hip broke, and the diagnosis gave him no more than two years to live. Tom was a great leader and friend, so this was a hideous development on every level. As I write this, we are one month from the 10th anniversary of his death, and I think about him every day. I'm either reminded of a lesson he taught or a joke he told. Mostly, I just miss him. Tom was one of those bosses with whom you could be a friend *and* employee.

Tom came back to the office for a few weeks after his diagnosis, but worked from home most of the time. When he called and asked that I come out to the house for a meeting, I thought nothing of it. It was a chance to catch up and talk about the strides our shows had made. And that's what it was until the end of our conversation when he asked, "What's the first thing you would fix with WIBC?"

Never shy to share my opinion, I said, "You need to fire Dave."

Dave "the King" Wilson had been the afternoon drive host on WIBC for 13 years. The show began as a showcase for Dave's amiable humor. He was a stand-up comedian featured on the syndicated Bob & Tom Show, and owned a comedy club and restaurant in Greenwood, just south of Indianapolis. His show was funny and topical — until September 11, 2001, the day of the attacks on the World Trade Center and Pentagon. That event demanded the show evolve into a news driven product, and that didn't fit Dave's strength. Dave wasn't as passionate about making people think as he was making them laugh, so the show lost its spark. I didn't see Jon, who was still the program director, steering Dave back toward humor, so I said replacing him made sense.

This kind of conversation was not unusual. Tom encouraged honesty, even if he was unlikely to agree with it. Bluntness was encouraged. There are some bosses I would never be that bold with, but over 15 years of working with and for Tom, he never acted impetuously or vindictively. To me, it was just a small part of a nice conversation.

I walked out of the meeting without regret or a second thought about what had transpired.

Three weeks later, I got another call from Tom. It was time for another meeting, although this felt a little ominous because he gave me no inkling what we would discuss. His tone was different, and the timing was a little odd. We would meet the next day at his house for lunch.

On the drive to Tom's house, I tried to figure out what he wanted. This felt like the kind of meeting where a change would be announced. Getting fired seemed a long shot, as 1070 the Fan was rolling and I knew Tom was happy with the station. Getting promoted seemed a long shot, too, as there was no open position for me to be promoted to. Then I thought, "Holy shit! He's going to make me program director of WIBC."

Tom sat in the chair he occupied for much of the time after his diagnosis and ate his steak salad from T.D. Alibi's. I'm not sure if I ate or not. My mind was not on food. I sat on the couch and Tom came straight to the point, "Tomorrow, you're going to become the program director for WIBC. I'll meet with Jon over here at noon to let him go. At the same time, you'll fire Dave Wilson. Are you good with that?"

My feeling during that moment was exactly like what I've felt being fired myself. I went numb and stopped hearing words. I'm sure I nodded or mumbled something, shook Tom's hand, and left. Tom mentioned a raise. I recalled the figures, so I assumed I heard everything else correctly.

As the silt in my brain settled, I realized three things: my friend and former boss was going to lose his job, my dream job of programming a news/talk and sportstalk at the same time was going to happen, and, last but not least, I was going to have to fire Dave. I was excited and I was nauseous. Back in the office, I went to the human resources generalist to make sure all of the paperwork was ready for Dave, and then hid the rest of the day. Facing Jon as I knew something he didn't — that I would replace him the following day — was too unpleasant to contemplate.

Firing people is never easy, but each instance is as unique as each employee who gets the ax. Those you fire for cause are easy because it's deserved. Firing those who no longer fit for financial reasons is difficult because they've done nothing to earn their fate, and they are usually paying the price for mismanagement. With both of those rationales, there is a clear objective purpose for the move that can be easily communicated. With a subjective issue like fit — as with Dave — it is especially difficult. Add that I didn't necessarily agree with the decision, and it was hellish.

No one being fired ever wants to hear any mutation of "This is very difficult for me," so there was none of that with Dave. Despite knowing and liking him for 13 years, I kept it short as HR always instructs, handed him his separation agreement, and thanked him. Not surprisingly, Dave was great about it. We shook hands as he left.

I have no doubt Dave was a goner regardless of my comment to Tom, but I have lived with the regret since then that I should have told Tom we simply needed to let Dave be Dave instead of demanding the host of WIBC's afternoon drive show be more newsy than funny.

As is always the case with radio, one employee's misery is another employee's joy. That axiom worked in this case as Steve Simpson slid easily into the afternoon drive slot. Steve was (and is) a master broadcaster who is a genius at simultaneously hosting and producing a radio show — particularly during severe weather or breaking news. Steve would be a trusted voice for the next five years until he was replaced, as all hosts eventually are.

I don't know how Tom's meeting with Jon went, but because I remained in my office and Jon never came to clean out his belongings, the office remained as he left it for a very long time. It was more than a little eerie. He had seats from a demolished baseball stadium, an old TV guide autographed by Johnny Carson, and many other knickknacks that were uniquely Jon's. None of them moved from where he left them for over a year.

Tom would fight his cancer for another four months before it finally took him from us.

From my own experience, I know a person you have fired never wants to hear the reasons behind the decision — after all it's never positive, right? But one afternoon four years after I fired Dave he came to my house. There was some confusion over the time of a party for Emmis expatriates Julie and I were hosting, and Dave and I wound up alone in my living room for an hour.

I still felt awful about the sequence of events that took his job, so I caved into self-indulgence and explained exactly how and why his ouster came. With every sentence, I felt more ridiculous. Again, as always, Dave was magnanimous and accommodating. That meeting brought no closure for me, and I doubt it lessened the unpleasantness for him, either. That's the thing about firings — no amount of good wishes, kind thoughts, and meandering explanations make it easier, even four years later.

As you'll read soon, I would be axed myself 10 months after Jon and Dave were fired. For those of you keeping score at home, that's four people gone who worked for the same radio station/company for 16, 15, 13, and 13 years. Between March 1, 2009 and January 4, 2010, one passed away, and three were fired. That's a bad run, even for radio.

Lessons learned:

1. Keep it quick when firing people. They hear nothing after learning what's happening. The sad fact is that firing is about achieving two results — the axed party neither sues nor exacts revenge against the company or its employees.

2. Always be honest with your boss, but understand you may be held accountable for your honesty.

3. Understand that life is a zero sum game for most of us. Joyous events are often followed by horrible moments, and horrible moments sometimes breed happy times. In rare circumstances, both come simultaneously.

4. There are days when management is fun — and there are others when it's painful as hell.

Finally my Turn — Fired from Emmis

"This isn't going to be a pleasant meeting," Charlie said as he closed the door to his office.

Charlie was the manager who replaced Tom two months after he passed away, and he was right. Over the next two minutes, Charlie put an end to my 16 years as a manager of talk radio programming with Emmis. And it was not pleasant.

It's not that anyone yelled or made obscene gestures, but firing people or being fired is a source of joy only for crazy people.

I knew, as I related in the previous chapter about firing Dave 'the King" Wilson, that the goal of a termination meeting is to ensure a lack of litigation or violence, so I accommodated management as the terms of my separation were outlined. All I wanted to do was leave, and I assumed that was all management wanted too.

But as Lee Corso says on ESPN's College Football Gameday, "not so fast my friend." As I stood and grabbed the folder with Cobra materials and my severance agreement, Charlie asked, "Don't you want to hear why?"

My brain screamed "Hell no!" My mouth quietly said, "Sure," as I returned to my seat. Ratings and revenue for both WIBC and 1070 the Fan were up, so that couldn't have been it, and if not that, what reason could possibly make any sense? Charlie made noises that sounded like words, but I heard none of them. All I could think of was how I would tell my wife and son about this turn of events. My son had three semesters of college left, and that meant approximately $48,000 in tuition and room & board needed to be found somewhere.

Even now I couldn't tell you what was said as I patiently made eye contact as his explanation was offered.

The last thing Charlie said was, "In time you'll see this is a very good thing for you."

My brain screamed, "Oh, so you're letting yourself off the hook by believing this is a favor you're doing for me?!" My mouth said, "Thanks, I appreciate that."

I knew the typical protocol was for me to leave the building immediately. They would prefer I return over the weekend for my personal stuff. No manager wants the distraction of some morose boob weeping as he or she says their final goodbyes as boxes are hauled to the elevator. I wanted nothing to do with theatrical bawling, but I did want to tell a few people goodbye. They meant too much to me to just leave them without a handshake or hug. It always seemed bizarre that fired staff members evaporated from our midst to never be seen again immediately prior to the email announcing their dismissal. Selfishly, I wanted to let people know that being fired was not going to break me.

I explained to Charlie what I planned, shook his hand, and left his office without giving him a chance to argue.

The first stop was the CEO's office. Jeff Smulyan has always been a good guy, and more importantly an honest guy. I liked him when I worked for him, and I like him today. When I walked into his office on the seventh floor, Jeff said, "Kent, there's nothing I can do."

That he thought I would grovel to him to try to save my job pissed me off. I had been through this on the other end a dozen times, and I knew Jeff never involved himself in personnel matters. Plus, even if he would have interceded, why would I want to work for a manager who wanted someone else at my desk? Emmis had always been quite fair with me, so I had no complaint for Jeff. "I'm not here for that," I snapped. "I want to thank you for 16 wonderful years. I had a great time."

I shook his hand and I left.

After I said goodbye to some of the rest of the staff, I got in the car and began the drive to Julie's office. I had no idea how she might take the news, so I called Paulie Balst, my old friend from Indiana University and a few subsequent years in Chicago. He told me the same thing the manager did, "This is the best thing that could happen for you. You need to start writing. Launch a website today. Don't wait. Do it today, and write your ass off. You don't need a job to work, and you should have been a writer anyway."

I called Rob Nichols, a tech savvy friend with whom I had worked at Emmis, and asked how difficult it would be to launch a website. He told me he would put one together quickly. All that got done on the 30-minute drive from the Emmis Building to Julie's office, so at least I had a next step to present to Julie when I told her of my gassing.

There had been some quiet maneuvering by Charlie that signaled my time at Emmis would soon be over. But I kept working like hell to show my value as I foolishly believed his mind could be changed. Charlie was — and is — intensely loyal to those who previously worked for him, and being replaced by members of his team was an inevitability regardless of my dogged efforts.

No shame in being replaced if your work is good, but trying to tell that to Julie seemed self —serving and trivial. The severance would take care of our immediate cash needs, but this was still a jarring development. As I walked into Julie's office, she could see in my eyes that something was different. I told her I had been fired. She replied, "I'm sorry for you."

That was odd. Julie doesn't care for change, and this was a profound change. I had worked for WIBC or Emmis since before we moved to Indianapolis from Chicago. I explained the construction of the website, and how I wouldn't miss a day of work even if I wasn't working for Emmis anymore. She smiled.

I was baffled by her reaction. As I drove home, I tried to make sense of the smile. That didn't seem like Julie at all. I assumed that she would need to be comforted, but she actually seemed relieved.

Finally, I dismissed it. The smile must have been in my imagination.

Four days later, Julie came home from work, and said we needed to talk. For the next 20 minutes, she explained why she had smiled. While I had immersed myself in the work of programming WIBC and 1070 the Fan, I had ignored her. She had decided it might be time to split, and had planned to have a different conversation prior to my being canned.

She said, "As soon as you got fired, the you I married was back. I just want to tell you that you being fired might be a bad thing for you, but it's a very good thing for us."

In every English class I had ever taken, the lesson was the same, "Write what you know." What I knew in that moment was that getting fired sucked, so that was the topic of the first post at *kentsterling.com*.

I wrote about any subject on which I had a coherent thought. Quickly, I honed in on sports. Sports is too frivolous to stir up a hornets nest of hate with every keystroke, and it has always been my passion. Politics was too serious, and having a coherent and logical conversation about topics as divisive as health care reform, the electoral college, Iraq and Afghanistan, or gun control is impossible. I learned that lesson at the kitchen table when I was a child.

My lament over losing my job evaporated, although I continued to feel bad about the direction the stations were headed. In my mind, we were building something special, and I wanted to continue that work.

Looking back, as much as it galls me to admit it, Charlie was right. Rarely does a firing turn out well for everyone, but in this case it did. The challenge of writing and talking about sports continues to stimulate me every day. My marriage is stronger than ever. Ryan not only got his undergrad degree with a double major, but also earned his law degree. Under Charlie, Emmis Indianapolis continued its positive momentum and he was promoted to run the New York cluster of Emmis stations. The managers who stood by Charlie during the tough period he endured prior to joining Emmis have established themselves as successes.

Sometimes, everybody wins.

Lessons learned:

1. Don't overreact to momentary setbacks. Overcoming adversity requires resolve, and sometimes that means denying the impulse toward self-pity.

2. Embrace change. It's inevitable, so understand positive change and negative change sometimes impersonate one another.

3. Surrounding yourself with a network of friends who can see beyond the pain to offer constructive guidance can be the key to maintaining work ethic and sanity.

Driving Mr. Boyle

Getting lunch with smart people is something I enjoy. That in itself is not a mistake. I recommend it highly. However, the ideas hatched during these lunches can cause problems. My lunch with Mark Boyle a few years ago led to a series of colossal blunders.

Boyle is the radio play-by-play voice of the Indiana Pacers, and he is exceptionally smart. His story is fascinating, and so a sandwich asking him about some of his life decisions was a lot of fun. Knowing what he wanted to do with his life as a teen, Boyle never felt the need to attend college. His dad was an outstanding broadcaster, and that is exactly what he wanted his career to be.

As he became a professional, Boyle decided he would give himself until he turned 30 to become the voice of a major league team regardless of the sport. He knocked around for a few years in small markets, and then came to New York and St. Louis as a talk host before landing the gig with the Pacers after turning 29, barely beating his self-imposed deadline.

After being hired in Indianapolis, Boyle did a little cursory research into the ages of the play-by-play talent in the NBA, and he was the youngest by far in the league. Maybe his deadline was a little demanding, but arguing with that level of success would be ridiculous.

I consider Boyle the best radio play-by-play talent in America — in any sport. He prepares relentlessly, has a very solid understanding of the game of basketball, and has developed a chemistry with Bobby "Slick" Leonard that has made listening to Pacers games a pleasure for more than 30 years.

He might argue, but I think he could do a great job of calling football or hockey, and I know he can do baseball because during one of his summer adventures, he broadcast some split-season single-A baseball in Montana. As an NBA voice he gets summers off, which leads to a question I asked during our lunch that I would come to regret.

"What do you have going on this summer?" I asked.

"I'm walking through Indiana, 500 miles all over the state," he replied. Indeed, he would walk 25-30 miles a day for four weeks to raise money for the Indiana Children's Wish Fund.

"What can I do to help?" I asked.

"We need drivers for the RV, if you're game," Boyle dared.

I told him that sounded like fun, which was true because everything sounds like fun to me four weeks before I have to do it. The commitment seemed manageable — drive to the next stop every day so Boyle wouldn't have to carry all his stuff around the state on this adventure. How hard could driving an RV be?

A normal person might have tried to assess his ability to drive an RV before tackling the challenge, but I had driven 22-foot U-Hauls many times as well as a full-blown tractor trailer through the streets of Chicago. This couldn't be much tougher than that, right?

On June 21st, I met Boyle and the RV at a campground just south of Indianapolis. My wife looked at me with a level of doubt and confusion that was more than justified. The RV was enormous — kind of like a tour bus. Boyle gave us a quick tour, and not surprisingly the responsibilities of driving a house on wheels were just a bit more involved than driving a short U-Haul.

Even more troubling than Julie's look of dire concern was the news that the driver who volunteered the previous week bolted when he saw the size of the motor home. I knew the guy to be very smart, and if he bounced maybe that would be the right thing for me to do as well.

Among the myriad of differences between this beast and any four-wheeled vehicle you or I might have driven, this RV had four hydraulic lifts that level the home when stationary, which need to be retracted for it to roll. Also, stairs need to be deployed for climbing in and out, an emergency brake is not optional when at rest, and — most troubling — the portable sewage tank needs to be emptied daily. You can guess what needs to be expelled from the tank.

Boyle walked me around what we would call home for the next five days and informed me that among my responsibilities would be hooking one end of the giant hose to the valve connected to the tank and snaking the other into the septic tank at the campground. I said nothing to Boyle at the time, but two things were not going to happen during our journey through the back roads of southern Indiana. I would not be responsible for any portion of the sewage that would need to be emptied. My deposits would be made in restrooms at campsites and restaurants. And two, I would not be emptying Boyle's waste under any circumstance.

Julie got in the car, waved sadly, and drove away. I thought her melancholy came from a place of missing me. I found out later it was the result of understanding that somehow, some way, this was not going to end well.

My senior year of college at Indiana, friends who had already graduated loaded into an RV and bombed down to Bloomington for the Little 500 weekend. Little 500 is a huge celebration and party with a 200 lap bicycle race as the centerpiece, and our friends were ready for mayhem. After the race, 45 of us piled into the RV as it rolled to a stop on State Road 46 because of traffic. There was a thin strip of a shoulder to the right of our lane, and our driver Goofy Mike hit the gas and passed dozens of cars going dangerously fast. "You don't see an RV do this very often!" Goofy Mike yelled as he laughed.

He pulled into the gravel parking lot at Memorial Stadium and did donuts as the parents of some of our friends clung to the card table bolted to the floor and turned green.

That was the extent of my RV experience as passenger or driver as Boyle and I began our adventure.

Boyle took off walking in his yellow reflective vest and flannel pajama bottoms adorned with the image of Stewie from "Family Guy." He was quite a sight.

My most egregious mistake during our week together betrays me as a moron. I assumed the motor home was meant to be navigated everywhere a car could go. Because I do not travel in, around, or with motor home people, it never occurred to me some places were not meant for RVs. I found one of those places in Nashville, Indiana, on day four.

The goal was to park in a lot where I had seen some school buses. I had no GPS, so I had to eyeball my way through Nashville — a town filled with antiques, both in furniture and humanity. The buses were to my west, so I took a small street in that direction. This took me into a parking lot for Casa del Sol, a restaurant not connected to the lot where the buses parked. By the time I knew what I was doing I was pot-committed to continuing forward. Turning the RV around was impossible, and backing out was way too big a challenge for a novice like me.

A voice yelled, "Whoa! Whoa! Whoa!" I stopped immediately and climbed out of the RV. An elderly fellow looked at me with utter disdain, "What the hell are you doing?"

"I'm trying to get to that lot over there," I answered.

"This lot doesn't go there. This is a restaurant parking lot," he said, stating the very obvious. "You're rubbing up against Jimmy's car."

He was right. The RV was in contact with a 10-year-old sedan. I asked the old guy to guide me a little as I backed out. By the time I cleared the RV from Jimmy's car, a small crowd of elderly diners had gathered. "You hit Jimmy's car!" people chanted, not quite in unison, but with definitive anger. I heard rumbles from people saying I was fleeing the scene before they stopped me.

I tried to calm them. "I have insurance, and I was only moving the RV to get it away from the car. I have insurance. No need to worry."

Jimmy, the car's owner, came running out of the restaurant in a panic. He was also mentally challenged. The elderly and angry throng were vocal, and not helping Jimmy maintain his emotional well-being during my explanation of the events that led to a baseball sized smudge on his rear bumper. I told Jimmy I would move the RV to a place where traffic in and out of the restaurant would not be blocked, and then I would return to share my information with him. Then I explained to the growing masses of do-gooders that I would extract the RV, and would return. A solid dozen of them shuffled to the rear of the RV to copy the license plate number, and then formed a network of guides all yelling "right" and "left" simultaneously.

Somehow, I got out without causing any more damage and drove to a park three blocks west. Maybe a minute after I put the RV in park, two police cars rolled up alongside. One of the cops asked, "Are you the guy who hit Jimmy's car?" After I told them I was, they wanted to know why I left the scene of an accident. They also wanted the insurance papers from the RV. I had no idea what those papers looked like or where to find them, but I told them I had explained my decision to leave and return to a group of 70-80 octogenarian Mexican food fans who gathered at the scene of the horror.

My chief concern wasn't the police. It was Jimmy. I didn't want him to think I had abandoned ship. The police kept going through the cabinets, and finally found a rental agreement. With that straightened out, I ran back to the restaurant and assured Jimmy everything would be taken care of. Through finding the contract, we discovered the RV was fully insured. Thank God. Probably should have figured that out on the front end of the trip.

The rest of the trip was filled with minor bloopers — like my not securing my new iMac for a quick drive to a McDonald's in Columbus. I rolled the back wheels over a curb, and the computer fell, smashing the screen. I left the emergency brake disengaged for several hours in Bloomington, and fortunately the pavement at the campground was perfectly level. It never moved. If it had, the limits of the insurance would likely have been tested. In an act of total idiocy beyond my ability to defend, I bent the stairs leading to the RV by driving them into a tree.

There was not a single moment navigating that beast when I was at peace. Throughout the entire journey, I was terrified I would destroy the machine or people around it. The week was an exercise in discombobulation. Boyle seemed to be mostly unaware of my buffoonery as he was walking while I careened.

We met a woman along the way who fascinated Boyle by claiming that she had lived in every one of America's 50 states. It was interesting to listen to the interview the endlessly curious Boyle conducted. All they needed were microphones and a transmitter, and it would have been a great 90 minutes of radio.

My responsibilities ended on a Saturday afternoon, and I have never felt so happy about getting behind the wheel of a car. They are far easier to maneuver than 45-foot RVs.

Julie picked me up, and agreed that we should never become RV people. Given the publication of these stories, no insurance company in the world would ever underwrite a policy for me as a driver anyway. Julie asked, "How'd you like emptying the tank?" I laughed, and told her I never emptied it. She asked if I thought that was fair. I assured her I never put anything in there that needed to be emptied.

Julie asked why. I responded, "I don't have a lot of rules in my life, but I refuse under all circumstances to drive my own poop around."

Lessons learned:

1. There is a missing piece to the actors' axiom, "If you're asked if you can ride a horse, say yes." It is between the moment actors say yes and the time at which they have to saddle up that they need to develop some horse-riding skill. Not sure where I would have taken RV driving lessons, but they couldn't have hurt.

2. When volunteering to help someone for any reason and duration, asking whether there are any tasks involving a septic tank or poop is reasonable.

3. Driving an RV in a small town is like trying to pilot a golf cart from your bedroom to the kitchen in a two-story house.

Meet Me in St. Louis

My phone began blowing up on a May morning in 2011. A job as a program director had opened in St. Louis at an outstanding sports talk station, and people thought I would be right for it.

I respected each of the people who called, so I phoned the general manager of the station and expressed my interest.

For the previous 16 months, I had worked hard to establish a brand as a writer and show host in Indianapolis after spending the previous 17 years in radio management, so this would be a step in a different direction if they offered me the job — and if I accepted it.

I was happy writing, hosting, and becoming an early adapter of social media, but there were a few residual issues that remained from my being fired from Emmis Communications in 2010. As is the case with most people who are fired, I felt my termination was unjust — a move entirely unrelated to my performance as a program director. Ratings were good — and improving. Revenue was good — and improving. And, WIBC had won both a Marconi and Crystal Award a few months before I got the boot.

There was a gnawing desire in me to prove wrong the man responsible for my ouster, and if I could be convinced that I would have the resources necessary to help build

101ESPN into the #1 station in St. Louis — and if the money was right — it would be a sweet opportunity.

The more I listened to the radio station and followed the staff's work online, the better I felt about how motivated the ownership was to get things right. There were a few obvious flaws, but overall this was a really solid station with an understanding of how to deliver a great product.

I agreed to an interview, and enjoyed it in large part because of the presence of a guy who had programmed the best talk station I ever heard — The Loop in Chicago. Greg Solk managed a lineup with radio legends Jonathan Brandmeier, Kevin Matthews, Steve Dahl & Gerry Meier, Chet Coppock, Ed Tyll and Danny Bonaduce. If you were a guy living in Chicago in your 20s when that station was at its peak, this was what you listened to — all day. It was a magical station where shows flowed together in a seamless and hilarious day-long romp. The Loop is still my favorite all-time radio station.

Getting a chance to talk radio with Solk was something I looked forward to on my drive to St. Louis, and I wasn't disappointed. The interview, which also included market manager John Kijowski and consultant Rick Scott, was enjoyable. We talked about all kinds of things during our 90 minutes, and I left feeling they were going to offer me the job.

I have a quirk that doesn't help much in these situations — the feeling that a job offer is a win, and declining it shows a lack of respect for those making the offer. That makes me a terrible negotiator, I realize, but I feel this compulsion to agree to terms because I don't want to appear to be a dick.

Kijowski gave me an idea when a decision would be made, so Julie and I discussed the salary necessary to justify making a move from a city we enjoy to one we were mostly unfamiliar with. When the call came to offer the job, I had a specific dollar figure in mind. When Kijowski made the offer it was exactly the number Julie and I agreed would suit our needs. Without a reason to say no, I agreed to take the gig right there on the phone.

Sterlings are well known — at least within our family — for putting the cart before the horse, and that was the case here. When Julie tried to give notice to her boss, he said it was out of the question. Julie was not prepared for that, and we began a series of discussions to figure out whether I was premature in accepting the job.

Our conclusion was to split. Julie would stay in Indianapolis and I would move to St. Louis. Julie would drive to St. Louis every weekend because a program director doesn't stop managing the product on Saturdays and Sundays. We assumed the people of St. Louis and Indianapolis would be roughly the same. The two cities are only separated by 244 miles. How different could they be?

We learned soon after moving that St. Louis was more than a little bit different. Many of the people in Indianapolis have moved from somewhere else, and there is a pervasive friendliness. Hoosier Hospitality is a real thing. There is no such thing as Missouri Hospitality. In St. Louis, virtually everyone was born and raised there. They ask where you went to high school as a societal test. We met several people eager to welcome us, but the overall vibe was that we were outsiders visiting on some kind of domestic visa. St. Louis is a southern river town that has little in common with its neighbors to the east.

There is also an overt racism in the city that we found appalling. The riots in Ferguson were inevitable. Even people I believed to be reasonable had no issues expressing disdain for cultural, racial, and religious differences.

Early in my time at 101ESPN, I made two mistakes. At the meeting where I introduced myself to the staff, I made my first. It was ridiculous. Bernie Miklasz was our midday host — a major presence in St. Louis as the lead sports columnist for the *St. Louis Post-Dispatch*. I had googled him, seen a picture, and assumed because the guy who sat to my left was the guy in the picture that he was Miklasz. I welcomed him to the meeting by name, "I'm not who you think I am," the fellow said.

"I'm Brendan Shanahan, your imaging director."

Good God. I knew that no matter what I said after that, the takeaway in the halls after the meeting would be that I called Shanny "Bernie."

The second mistake came a couple of weeks later. The station brought in a professional photographer and make-up person to create head shots for all the talent and management. Hosts came in and got spray tan on their faces, eyebrows waxed, and eyeliner applied. I watched former professional athletes go through this process prior to me, so I adapted to my surroundings. I allowed the make-up person to do whatever she thought was best. I closed my eyes, went to my happy place, and tried not to pay attention.

The pictures were taken, and I ran to a meeting with some corporate big wigs immediately after. Roughly 30 minutes into my presentation on the financial health of the department, I wondered what I looked like with all the make-up and spray tan. My performance became fractured as my focus shifted from my department's finances to stark terror that I looked like a drag queen (not that there is anything wrong with that).

I stumbled to the end, was dismissed from the meeting. and ran to the men's room to check a mirror. Yep, I looked absurd. My skin tone was pumpkin-esque, and the edges of my eyelids were obviously caked in mascara. I stuck my face in the sink under running water and scrubbed like hell. It took 10 minutes to get my face back to a normal flesh tone.

I ran back to the conference room and interrupted the next presentation, "I just thought it was important to share that I came straight to our meeting from getting my head shot taken, and there were cosmetics involved. *That* is not how I normally present myself in a business proceeding." Thankfully, everyone laughed.

The staff was as good as in any sports talk station in America. I made tweaks throughout my two years in St. Louis, and the staff executed exceptionally well. 101ESPN jumped to #1 toward the end of my first year there. I like to think I had something to do with it, but the truth is the Cardinals run to the 2011 World Series Championship was a nice piece of serendipity that spiked our growth.

Julie made the drive between Indy and St. Louis every weekend. We found a restaurant we liked, and treated every weekend like a mini-vacation. Our time in St. Louis was a great check-up for our marriage. If there was any sense that being together wasn't worth it, those drives would have become intolerable. What was intolerable were the days and nights we were apart.

I had two primary goals in St. Louis. The first was to help the staff learn to truly enjoy their jobs. They were already working harder than any group I had ever heard of, so cracking the whip would have been counterproductive. I can be a disciplinarian, but that was not necessary with that group. The second was to ensure that when I returned to Indy from St. Louis (which was inevitable because remaining a dual residence couple was not a long-term solution, and our marriage is more important than a job) the assistant program director would be tabbed as the program director.

Hoss Neupert was my assistant, and having been a long-suffering assistant PD myself, I can tell you that no APD in the history of radio has been more supportive of a boss than he was. I enjoyed his friendship and partnership. We had a lot of laughs, made some needed changes, and worked through a cluster of relentless health-related adversity to the staff.

Feeling both had been accomplished, plus getting the station briefly to the No. 1 ranking, it was time to move home to Indy. The station has thrived for the past six years under Hoss's leadership, and the staff still sounds great.

Julie is thrilled she no longer has to make that drive and hear people spew racist comments, and is relieved that a significant portion of our debt was resolved.

After I returned, I picked up where I left off with *kentsterling.com* and was granted a second shot at the weekend radio show Chris Hagan and I hosted on 1070 the Fan, (which led to a five-year run for me on CBS Sports 1430). I also became a full-time husband again. And, I came back with a deeper understanding that Indianapolis had somehow become home to a kid from Chicago, which is a hell of a thing to learn.

This is a book about learning from mistakes, and while that move did cost me two years of my life, I have a tough time categorizing the move to St. Louis as a mistake. We were certainly less than diligent in making the decision to take the job, but I regret little about the experiences I had there. It just wasn't home, and the time came when it was impossible to justify the sacrifices my family made for the privilege of working with a lot of good people for a nice chunk of change in a difficult town.

Lessons learned:

1. Geographic proximity is not a predictor of attitudinal simi-
larities.

2. Until you meet a person, don't refer to him by name.

3. What some cosmetologist says will make you look good
in a photo doesn't translate well in a meeting.

4. Indianapolis is an underrated city, and St. Louis is rated
correctly.

An Event So Special, It's a Mistake to Write About It

This is the final chapter, because my inability to adequately describe how I met Julie is my greatest and most regrettable mistake.

I'm just terrible at telling the story of how we met, became a happy couple through the highs and lows of 35 years together, and combined to create a wonderful son. This is a book about mistakes, and God knows we have made our share over those years. We continue to challenge each other on a daily basis, and always find a way to embrace or overcome them. Julie is a huge part of what makes me tolerable as a human being. Sometimes I punch the gas and she steers. Occasionally, Julie goes fast and I navigate. Neither of us has much of a brake system.

We make life fun for each other, and never allow a day to be boring or end angry. Her ability to empathize astounds me, and my growth as a human being who can value the good in others rather than reject their flaws is almost entirely due to her example.

My inability to tell our story is because I am incapable of pulling back far enough to see it without feeling it, and sadly I am not skilled enough to articulate my feelings with the precision and grace Julie deserves.

I've tried to write this chapter at least 20 times. It's enjoyable to fail at it because it gives me another excuse to take a look back at moments that were both routine and spectacular — with a woman who is remarkable in every way. Julie's passion for learning, improving, loving, and listening is a benchmark almost impossible to reach. She is the Mount Everest of humanity. No one tries harder, nor succeeds more often at reaching people and showing them the love they deserve. Everyone should have Julie in their lives. I'm the lucky one who both figured that out and convinced Julie our life together might be fun.

If only for posterity, I'll try again to tell you how we met, and how quickly we decided spending the rest of our lives together would be a dance worth sharing.

Speaking of dancing, here's how we met...

"Don't screw this up! She's the one!" That's what Freddy yelled at me over Bob Seger's *Rock and Roll Never Forgets* at a party my first senior year in apartment D-19 at Walnut Knolls in Bloomington, on August 30, 1984. I had been dancing with an energetic sophomore named Julie Purcell for 15 minutes when Freddy made his proclamation. He was 12 minutes late. I already knew.

For years, like everyone else, I had wondered two things — would I ever bump into the woman I was meant to spend my life with, and would I be smart enough to know it when I did? That night I got the answers to both questions. On that Thursday night, when Julie and I danced for the first time, I knew she was the one.

That dance is best described as a shot of Elwood Blues (Dan Aykroyd's character in *The Blues Brothers*), a teaspoon of R&B legend Jackie Wilson, and a dash of spinmastster Ann Miller. It was frenetic, improvisational, and exhausting, and for the better part of three hours we believed we were the only people in the room, and then literally were.

That night started like so many others — a few beers, music, and then dancing. D-Building in Walnut Knolls Apartments was a festive place in 1984. Somehow the stars aligned that fall, and 35 apartments filled with friendly, funny, and thirsty Indiana University students. Our building was like a two-semester summer camp. It was a fraternal place without being a fraternity — exactly what any college kid would want. It was during that late August weekend which ran up to the beginning of classes that three of the six roommates in D-19 found the men they would marry, and it was another roommate named Lori who kind of introduced us by saying, "Julie, you've got to come see this guy out there. He dances just like you."

Julie left her bedroom conversation with a roommate, and by the end of the night we fell asleep on the couch locked together as we have been for 35 years.

Ten nights later, over a mammoth jug of wine, I said, "You know, I think we should get married." Julie replied that the timing might be a little squirrelly. I agreed and said, "Well, not today, but someday."

Julie said, "Well, okay," and two years and nine months later we made good on the promise of that night.

I don't recommend that timeline for everyone, but it was perfect for us. I would rather be a part of a relationship or business that does the right thing at the wrong time rather than the wrong thing at the right time, and Julie and I wrote the rulebook on doing the right thing at the wrong time in a way that allows it to come out exactly right. There is no flow chart for a perfect marriage, and that's a good thing because we both suck at flow charts.

That semester was interrupted by Julie's decision to leave school and return home to have her tonsils removed and try to re-engage her thirst for academia. The tonsillectomy was successful; the academics proved more difficult. Indiana University is a huge place with up to 400 students in a classroom. It's easy to get lost there. For those who need a personal touch from a professor, IU provides a challenge.

When Julie came back to Bloomington, we kind of majored in each other. I make no apologies for that; Julie is what made my six years of college (one short of *Animal House's* John Blutarsky) worthwhile. We needed to work together to get by, and if that's all we got out of our respective college experiences, it was well worth the effort.

We spent a fun summer together at IU and then one more academic year before finally saying goodbye to Bloomington.

The summer was great fun. I got a job at the Pizza Hut across the street from our apartment complex as the opening cook. It was my job to prep all the crust and sauce from scratch for the day's pies. That took three hours, starting at 8 a.m. At 11 a.m. when we opened, I cooked the personal pan pizzas for the lunch crowd. It was monotonous work, as you can imagine, but the thing that made me hate it most was the juke box. Every half hour, the machine would blare a song to remind customers it was there. This happened whether the restaurant was open or closed, so weekdays from 8 a.m. to 11 a.m., it scared the hell out of me six times.

After three weeks, I had enough. On that Friday after the lunch rush ended, I told the manager I was going to take out the garbage. I did, and then I just kept going. Julie asked what I was doing back at the apartment. "I left," I told her. She nodded, said OK, and we enjoyed an afternoon at the pool. A week later I returned to the restaurant and asked for my paycheck. The manager was astonished, and asked, "Where did you go? We were so worried." I told her I stopped having fun, so I left. Her facial expression morphed from confused sympathy to red-faced anger. "Not having fun? *What*? Here's your check."

With that episode, I discovered Julie was OK with abject irresponsibility. She knew I was a work in progress, and that was all right by her. If I needed any confirmation Julie was the woman for me, that was it. For a long time I dealt with tedium by abruptly removing myself from it.

We decided to take a sabbatical from Bloomington to go camping in Shenandoah National Park. This was Julie and I at our best. We had no car and no camping equipment, but were resourceful, if totally irresponsible. I had received a credit card from Sears with a limit of $260 I never asked for, so we bought exactly $260 in camping equipment, rented a tent, and stopped by Ugly Duckling to see about a car. They had one set of wheels they were willing to let us rent for $9 per day without a credit card. We checked every high risk box, and they still rented us the car. Incredibly, Ugly Duckling is still in business.

The only catch was that the car was a silver 1974 Ford Pinto with a manual transmission and enough cosmetic damage to make protecting it from the elements unnecessary. Neither of us had ever driven a stick, but I was undaunted. How hard could it be, and how better to learn than in a $200 car? Nothing like the logic of college students in love. We hit the road.

The Shenandoah Mountains were beautiful. We talked about life, argued, slept, found dozens of deer, never saw a bear, were frozen in place for a half-hour by a skunk outside the restrooms, and returned with the car, tent, and equipment intact. That trip served as a snapshot of how we would operate for the next three decades — decide what's best, and then do it with enthusiasm and only a quick glance at the consequences.

Even after 35 years, Julie has never become boring, and I have made significant strides in my ability to adapt to routine if not monotonous responsibilities.

Some get married and stay together. Some marry and divorce. Others never get married. There is no correct answer as to how a life is best lived — each life has unique challenges and solutions. Some yearn to correct their parents' errors, and others plot to repeat their successes. Julie and I have done things our own way, because that's all we have ever known. We dance to the beat of our own drummers, because it is all we have ever heard. Those drums don't always beat in unison, but to hope they might is silly.

There have been many moments of self-doubt that I navigated because at least I was smart enough to recognize Julie as the person I would love for the rest of my life. There must be something decent about me because, after all the flakiness and occasional departures from reason, here she is.

I wish I was a perfect husband for Julie, an inexhaustible reservoir of consideration and kindness, but that would waste Julie's estimable ability to tolerate foolishness and idiocy. She brings out the best in me, and makes me feel like I must have a purpose — or why would she have stuck around for 35 years?

Lessons learned:

1. Keep writing until you get it right, and even if it isn't perfect stand by the best you can do.

2. If you're incapable of genius, trust your stupidity — at least it's yours.

3. When you feel love, embrace it.

4. Driving a stick is best learned in a rental.

5. Don't charge camping supplies. I didn't mention this, but we finished paying off the Sears card in 1988, making our camping trip the most expensive vacation we ever took.

Epilogue

Writing this book was a weird experience. Revisiting memories brought both joy and pain. Many of the people in these stories have died and I miss them. As I wrote, their presence was very real — which brought joy. That their days of bringing love and laughs to others has ended is incredibly sad.

I thought of my dad a lot, heard his voice, and remembered what it was like to have him around on a daily basis. Dad was a character, but he was also courageous, loyal, and modest. He didn't invite praise or love, and so I rarely gave him a lot of positive feedback. I wish I had. As I wrote about his sitcom-esque moments, I repeatedly recalled the conversation he and my mom had shortly before he died. He asked her, "I guess we did okay, right?" I wish I had told him I wouldn't change a thing, and that he has four outstanding grandchildren because of the love and lessons he and Mom instilled in my sister and me. I wish I knew he would have liked to have heard that.

People have asked what writing a book is like. I would describe it as being similar to running a marathon. There is no point at which it is not a grind, but there is also a great satisfaction in making the effort. It's a solitary exercise that is incredibly tense — especially in the editing and proofreading. This book will outlive me, and if my words are not correctly chosen and assembled it will not reflect who I am or was, and that is the whole point.

I made a decision to share the actual names of some people in the book and not those of others. Embarrassing anyone — other than myself — was not my intent, so I tried to put myself into the shoes of those recalled in this book. If my description might shame them or their descendants, I changed their names. My third grade teacher's name was altered because I mentioned that she drunk-dialed my parents repeatedly. She has almost certainly passed away, but her children and grandchildren are likely not eager to read about her in that light. The name of my first college roommate was changed as well because of his drug use. No point in sharing that kind of detail about a guy who has either changed his ways or died.

It would be great if those who read these book learn from my mistakes, but I know from my own experience it's unlikely. If these stories help people find their own mistakes less loathsome, that would be a big win. People naturally want to be defined by their successes, but it is their failures that carve a direct path to triumphs. Fear of admitting temporary failure runs rampant in our society. Running from mistakes is not only fruitless; it's not fun. There is nothing that livens a dinner party conversation like the recollection of an embarrassing moment.

Embrace mistakes. Share them. Laugh at them. Learn from them. Understand the adversity that springs from mistakes brings our real education. Humility is a quality that should be celebrated, not derided as quaint and foolish.

Acknowledgements

Thanks to everyone I've ever met. Seriously. Even the jerks, tools, and lummoxes that have crossed my path have taught me something.

My sister deserves special mention because she is one of my greatest regrets. I should have been a much better brother, and I'm so sorry I wasn't. That's a mistake that didn't make it into the book. It could be its own book.

My late boss Tom Severino served as a bit of a role model for me in writing this book because he wrote one too — an intimate look at his life that exists only for family consumption. After Tom passed away, his wife Linda allowed me to read it, and it was incredible. The writing is so reminiscent of Tom that I could hear his voice as I read it. Because Tom did it, I felt like I should. Ten years after his passing, he's still a hell of a role model.

Mark Montieth has been generous enough to walk me through the process of writing and editing the book, and it would not exist in the form it does without his selflessness. As you glide effortlessly over the correctly spelled words in sentences that are well structured, thank Mark.

Most of us were fortunate to have a teacher who spoke to us as human beings and led us through tough times as an adolescent to more productive days as an adult. I had two of those. Kathy O'Hara was a history teacher at Lake Bluff

Junior High. I'm not sure how she knew kids so well, but when she spoke, we listened. She earned our respect through relentless honesty — both in words and emotion. Lee Kelly was my radio teacher in high school. He allowed me to learn about radio, develop a love for it, and help guide me periodically when I needed to be steered. Lee never turned his back on me when he would have been justified in doing so. Both Kathy and Lee were wonderful guides for kids who strayed from the beaten path.

My wife has been insanely generous in allowing me the time, space, and resources to do this as well as I am capable. As I mentioned many times in the book, Julie is incredibly selfless and supportive. She has always been exceptionally tolerant of my penchant for mistakes. Without them, this book (in much shorter form) would be nothing but a recitation of triumphs.

Thanks as always to my mom, who continues to be an enormous presence in all of our lives. She continues to learn, teach and love, and what could be better than that? I'm sorry that my behavior led to drunk-dials from a teacher, and that I was a challenge to parent. Maybe I should thank Mom for allowing me to screw up and learn endless lessons as a kid so that our son wouldn't have to repeat any of my foolishness.